D0042054

TWAYNE'S WORLD AUTHORS SERIES
A Survey of the World's Literature

SPAIN

Janet Pérez
Texas Tech University

EDITOR

Jorge Guillén

TWAS 641

Photograph by the Author

Jorge Guillén

JORGE GUILLÉN

By G. GRANT MacCURDY

California State University
Los Angeles

TWAYNE PUBLISHERS
A DIVISION OF G.K. HALL & CO., BOSTON

Published in 1982 by Twayne Publishers,
A Division of G. K. Hall & Co.

Printed on permanent/durable acid-free paper and bound
in the United States of America

First Printing

Library of Congress Cataloging in Publication Data

MacCurdy, G. Grant.
Jorge Guillén.

(Twayne's world authors series ; TWAS 641. Spain)
Bibliography: pp. 172–80
Includes index.
1. Guillén, Jorge, 1893– —Criticism and interpretation.
I. Title. II. Series.
PQ6613.U5Z76 861′.62 81–6726
ISBN 0–8057–6485–2 AACR2

For my teachers at the University of Arizona
Rupert C. Allen
Robert R. Anderson
A. Dolores Brown
Renato I. Rosaldo
H. Reynolds Stone
And to the memory of Charles F. Olstad

Contents

About the Author

Grant MacCurdy received his undergraduate education at the University of New Mexico, and his graduate degrees from the University of Arizona in Tucson. He is Professor of Spanish at California State University, Los Angeles, where he has taught since 1970. His articles on the poetry of Jorge Guillén are listed in the Bibliography.

Preface

During the first third of the twentieth century, Spanish letters achieved a flowering of excellence which the country had not experienced in three hundred years. The period is one of fertility in all the arts, and is especially remarkable for the wide-ranging works of several outstanding poets. More specifically, a group of poets known today as the Generation of 1927 consistently produced works of such quality that recent critics have written of a new Golden Age of Spanish literature.

The poet's poet, Jorge Guillén, is a key figure of this Spanish literary renaissance. Born at the end of the nineteenth century, Guillén began publishing poetry in the 1920s. In a period of unrestrained experimentation in literature, Jorge Guillén was recognized early in his career as a sculptor of finely wrought verse who avoided fashionable extremism in favor of a poetry that exhibited permanence in both form and thematic content. Furthermore, Guillén had no use for the nihilistic literary currents sweeping Europe in the wake of World War I. He called his first and most important work a hymnal, *Cántico* [Canticle], and in it he creates a resounding song of praise to life itself, to simple being as he the poet sees it.

The calamity of the Spanish Civil War and subsequent Falangist dictatorship caused the dispersal of the Generation of 1927 as a literary movement. Guillén's best-known contemporary, Federico García Lorca, died tragically and senselessly at the outset of the war, and most surviving members of the literary group left Spain for life in exile. Guillén emigrated to the United States, his permanent home from 1938 until after the death of Franco. Although a leading Spanish poet, Guillén has composed the bulk of his work while distant from his country and even his native language.

The intent in this volume is to begin to fill a serious void in criticism on Jorge Guillén for the English-speaking reader. There has not been a systematic study in English, an overview of his poetry, since 1942, when Guillén had published only about one tenth of the poetic works that have appeared to date. The lack of a general study in English is remarkable when one considers that

Guillén is a poet of global significance who lived in the United States for four decades, was a professor at several American universities, and has been translated into English three times in book-length editions.

After an introduction on Jorge Guillén and the Generation of 1927, the procedure in the chapters that follow is to survey and analyze Guillén's poetic works in chronological order. A chronological study will indicate the way in which Guillén begins his poetic career as an exponent of optimism and permanent human values, moves toward socially committed themes after the Spanish Civil War and World War II, then completes the circle by evolving in his later works toward a secure stance of poetic affirmation and joy that characterizes his earliest efforts.

Writing a short book about so vast a poetic effort—well over two thousand pages at present—involves some difficult decisions regarding allocation of space. Guillén's readers are virtually unanimous in the judgment that his first work, *Cántico,* is his most significant. This collective opinion is borne out by published criticism of the poet, which centers heavily on *Cántico*. Professor Guillén once remarked to me in conversation that he hoped future critics would not ignore his later works, then added half jokingly but not without a grain of truth, "pero con *Cántico* basta" ("but *Cántico* is enough"). With this in mind, about one half of the book is devoted to *Cántico* and its major themes. Guillén's second major work, *Clamor* [Clamor], is analyzed in a somewhat shorter chapter. The third major collection, *Homenaje* [Homage], constitutes a reaffirmation of the values of *Cántico*. As such, it is an important work for understanding the essential unity of Guillén's poetic vision, but can be characterized relatively briefly in a general study in which space is at a premium.

Guillén's fourth major work, *Y otros poemas* [And Other Poems], presents a special problem. Thematically, this collection has much in common with *Homage,* and for that reason it is discussed in the same chapter as being essentially a continuation of the previous work. There is a difficulty with the first (and only) edition of *And Other Poems* available in print at the present time. Guillén has always supervised quite closely the publication of his poetic works, even to the point of specifying the type size used in printing. Inexplicably, *And Other Poems* was published without the proofs being sent to the poet, the result being a book with several dozen printing errors. Some of these errata are minor and involve spelling, but others consist of misleading punctuation, and occasionally entire lines are omitted, interpolated, or misplaced. My copy of the text has the author's corrections, for which I am very grateful, and only poems which contain no errors are quoted. Professor Guillén is now publishing his collected poetry in definitive form, so the defective edition of *And Other Poems* should be superseded in the near future.

As one might expect of a poet who has also led a distinguished career as a professor of literature, Guillén has published criticism as well as poetry. I have had to limit discussion of Guillén's criticism to that relating to the Generation of 1927 and to his own poetry. His critical comments and evaluations appear in the discussions of his literary movement and specific works, and his most important prose works appear in the bibliography. It is the significance of Guillén's poetry that curtails the attention devoted to his prose.

Guillén's masterful control of language makes him a challenging poet to translate, but also a frustrating one—Guillén's work is approached with the somewhat disconcerting knowledge that his verse can never be adequately rendered into another language. The English versions that appear here should therefore be regarded as "working" translations in the sense that the poems are translated with accuracy of content as the primary objective—rhythm is a secondary consideration and rhyme disappears altogether. Some changes in phrasing and syntax are of course inevitable. Occasionally words or short phrases are added in brackets in order to clarify meaning. Also on occasion, a word or phrase translated in one way might have appeared in some other form. In such cases, which are relatively rare, the translator's apology must be that translation is the first step in interpretation, according to the reading of a given poem. All translations are my own, although I have freely consulted the published translations of Guillén's poetry.

One minor deviation in the translation of titles needs a word of clarification. The titles of Guillén's major collections translate easily, an exception being *Cántico*. This word means "hymnal" or "canticle," but *Cántico* is not religious poetry in any dogmatic sense, and the cognate "canticle" has a pedantic ring to it which does not do justice to Guillén's intention to compose an exuberant book of song to life. So I have left this title in Spanish, and it can be read as a "song of praise."

Many friends contributed to the realization of this book. Professor Jorge Guillén has been a kind and delightful guide—his warmth and brilliance are as apparent in his person as in his work. I also thank him for permission to quote from his works and personal letters. Three friends and colleagues, Professors Joseph A. Chrzanowski and Leon Schwartz of my own institution and Professor Andrew P. Debicki of the University of Kansas, were extremely generous in devoting their time to reading the manuscript and making valuable suggestions. My Twayne editor, Professor Janet W. Pérez was invariably gracious and always helpful with my queries and requests. My son, James Raymond, showed splendid patience for a ten-year-old while this project was being completed.

While poetic interpretation is necessarily a subjective and personal encounter to which poet and reader bring life experience and point of view, this study is of course meant to be an objective analysis of Jorge Guillén's poetry. Beyond that intended aim, I would like to add that Guillén's work has been a rich and profound well of inspiration to me through years of study and research. I sincerely hope that the reasons for my enthusiasm become objectively apparent and contagious in the chapters that follow.

A Note on the Titles

Jorge Guillén has carefully organized the different collections of his poetry, and his works present few bibliographic difficulties. However, readers who are unfamiliar with the development of Guillén's poetry may be confused by the plurality of titles which can refer to a single collection of poems.

For more than twenty years of his poetic career, Guillén published one book, *Cántico*, in successively larger editions. Following *Cántico*, the poet devoted himself to the development of *Clamor*. Like the previous collection, *Clamor* was published serially. Unlike *Cántico*, however, the three titles of verse which constitute *Clamor* bear separate titles: *Maremágnum* [Sea of Confusion], *Que van a dar en la mar* [We Will End at the Sea], and *A la altura de las circunstancias* [To Rise to the Occasion]. Therefore, a reference to any one of these collections should also be regarded as pertaining to *Clamor*. After *Cántico* and *Clamor*, Guillén published a third major work, *Homenaje*, issued as a single volume, for which reason references to it should not be confusing.

In 1968, Guillén published *Aire nuestro* [Our Air] in Milan, a compilation of the previous collections: *Cántico*, *Clamor*, and *Homage*. This massive volume has been the standard edition of the three works. Therefore, page references in the following chapters are to

Our Air, although the chapters themselves treat the various collections individually. To avoid confusion, parenthetical documentation includes the abbreviation *AN*, regardless of the specific collection being considered. Since *And Other Poems* is not part of *Our Air*, references to it are made separately. The relevant publication history of each collection is discussed in the respective chapters. Publication data appears in the bibliography.

Guillén has recently begun to publish his collected poetry in a new and definitive edition, also entitled *Our Air*. When complete, the multivolume set by Barral Editores will be the standard edition of Guillén's poetry. The page references of the present study will become "obsolete," in that the version of *Our Air* used here will be superseded by another edition. The new edition will contain an alphabetical index of poems, however, so readers of this and other studies of Guillén's works will not be inconvenienced by changes in pagination.

G. GRANT MACCURDY

California State University, Los Angeles

Chronology

1893	January 18, Jorge Guillén born in Valladolid, in Old Castile.
1903–1909	Secondary studies at the Institute of Valladolid.
1909–1911	Studies at the Maison Perreyve, Fribourg, Switzerland.
1911–1913	Studies at the University of Madrid, living at the Residencia de Estudiantes.
1913	At the University of Granada; receives licentiate in letters.
1913–1914	Resides in Halle and Munich, Germany.
1917–1923	Lecturer at the Sorbonne, Paris.
1920	Begins publishing in journals the poems later collected in *Cántico*.
1921	Marries Germaine Cahen in Paris.
1922	Birth of daughter Teresa in Paris (now Mrs. Stephen Gilman, Cambridge, Massachusetts).
1923	Death of mother, Esperanza Alvarez Guerra.
1924	Presents dissertation on Luis de Góngora and receives doctorate in letters from the University of Madrid. Birth of son Claudio in Paris.
1925	Successfully completes competitive examinations *(oposiciones)* for professorship in Spanish language and literature.
1926–1929	Professor of Spanish language and literature at the University of Murcia.
1928	Publishes the first edition of *Cántico*, containing seventy-five poems.
1929–1931	Lecturer in Spanish at Oxford University.
1931–1938	Professor at the University of Seville.
1934	Lectures in Romania.
1936	Publishes the second edition of *Cántico*, which contains 125 poems: July, the outbreak of hostilities of the Spanish Civil

War. August, the death by assassination of Guillén's friend and best-known contemporary, Federico García Lorca. September, Guillén arrested and detained in Pamplona as a political prisoner.

1938 Leaves Spain for voluntary exile in the United States.

1938–1939 Professor at Middlebury College.

1939–1940 Professor at McGill University.

1940–1957 Professor at Wellesley College.

1945 Publishes, with added subtitle, the third edition of *Cántico: Fe de vida* [Canticle: Testimony of Life], which contains 270 poems.

1947 Death of wife, Germaine. Visiting professor at Yale University.

1950 Publishes the fourth edition of *Cántico: Fe de vida*, the first complete edition, containing 334 poems. Death of father, Julio Guillén Sáenz. Visiting professor at the College of Mexico, Mexico City.

1951 Visiting professor at the University of California, Berkeley.

1952–1953 Visiting professor at Ohio State University.

1955 Award of Merit of the American Academy of Arts and Letters, New York.

1957 Publishes *Maremágnum* [Sea of Confusion], volume 1 of the poems collected in *Clamor: Tiempo de Historia* [Clamor: Time of History]. Poetry Prize of the City of Florence.

1957–1958 Charles Eliot Norton Professor of Poetry, Harvard University.

1959 Etna-Taormina Poetry Prize, Sicily.

1960 Publishes *Que van a dar en la mar* [We Will End at the Sea], the second volume of *Clamor*.

1961 Publishes *Language and Poetry: Some Poets of Spain* (a critical work expanding the lectures of Guillén's professorship at Harvard). Also publishes *El argumento de la obra* [The Theme of the Work], a critical essay on his poetry. Marries Irene Mochi Sismondi in Bogotá, Colombia. Visiting professor at the University of the Andes, Bogotá. International Grand Prize of Poetry, Belgium.

1962 Visiting professor at the University of Puerto Rico, where he also teaches in 1964 and 1970.

1963 Publishes *A la altura de las circunstancias* [To Rise to the Occasion], the third and final volume of *Clamor*.

1964 San Luca Prize, Florence.

1966 Visiting professor at the University of Pittsburgh.

1967 Publishes *Homenaje: Reunión de vidas* [Homage: A Gathering of Lives].

1968 Publishes *Aire nuestro* [Our Air], comprising *Cántico, Clamor,* and *Homage*. Guillén's seventy-fifth birthday is marked by a symposium at the University of Oklahoma.

1969 Publication of *Luminous Reality: The Poetry of Jorge Guillén* (anthology of essays consisting of the papers delivered at the Oklahoma symposium).

1973 Publishes *Y otros poemas* [And Other Poems].

1974 A symposium on Guillén's work at the University of Wisconsin.

1976 Miguel de Cervantes Prize of the Spanish Royal Academy, Madrid. Bennett Prize for Poetry of the *Hudson Review,* New York.

1977 Fetrinelli Prize of the Lincei Academy, Rome. Alfonso Reyes Prize, Mexico. Named *Doctor Honoris Causa* by the University of Valladolid.

1978 Guillén makes his permanent home in Málaga.

1981 Scheduled publication of *Final*.

CHAPTER 1

A Generation of Genius, 1920–1936

I *Background of the Generation of 1927*

As is the case with other European literatures, the nineteenth century in Spain is remembered as a particularly fertile period for the novel. Poetry in the late 1800s, however, is quite another matter. The poets who achieved considerable popularity during the second half of the century, notably Ramón de Campoamor and Gaspar Núñez de Arce, have proved of transient value in the view of most modern readers. On the other hand, the poets who are today most highly esteemed, the Galician Rosalía de Castro and Gustavo Adolfo Bécquer, received scant attention during their brief lifetimes. Toward the end of the past century, poetry was perhaps the least vital genre in Spanish literature. This stagnation makes the heights which Spanish lyrical expression was to achieve during the first third of the twentieth century all the more spontaneous and remarkable.

The first intimations of poetic renovation and eventual renaissance in Spain appear around the turn of the century in a series of distinct but related literary events, the first being the emergence of a group of writers later known collectively as the Generation of 1898. The year 1898 symbolizes an abysmal decline in Spanish national life, for that was the year of the Spanish-American War, in which Spain lost her last remaining overseas colonies, Cuba and the Philippines. From a world power in the sixteenth century, the country had become a literal and spiritual pauper, these writers felt, and in desperate need of (1) renovation from within its borders and (2) the introduction of new ideas from without. One immediate precursor of the group, Angel Ganivet, wrote that Spain was ahead of most nations in the natural cycle of evolution, for she had ascended to a peak, declined to a low ebb, and could only begin to rise again, the second time as a spiritual, not colonial, power.

Since the Generation of 1898 was concerned primarily with describing the Spanish "essence" and the problem of national life, the movement can be considered largely social in conception and orientation. The *Modernista* movement, aesthetic and primarily poetic, was simultaneously beginning to make itself felt in some circles.[1] By 1900, the Nicaraguan poet Rubén Darío had made his second trip to Spain and was influencing some younger writers. Darío is the best-known representative of Latin American modernism, an almost purely aesthetic movement that had as its goal the renovation of literary language and the accompanying creation of a poetic style of writing that could be applied to both poetry and prose. The language of modernism is rich in sensuous imagery, exoticism, and fantasy. Modernist poetry is far removed from the workaday world and typically displays an "ivory tower" mentality on the part of the poet (the "ivory tower" being a phrase used to characterize the exclusively aesthetic attitude of the authors who followed Darío's example).

Historically, Darío's most important contacts in Spain were with Antonio Machado (1875–1939) and the still adolescent Juan Ramón Jiménez (1881–1958). In view of their later development, the influence of Darío may have been more incidental than decisive, but he was an inspiration to these young poets who would themselves be influential leaders for a time to the poets who blossomed in the 1920s. Jiménez and Machado were regarded as the leading poets in Spain when Jorge Guillén, Federico García Lorca, Pedro Salinas, and others were embarking on their literary careers shortly after World War I. Their poetry of profound introspection and vividly meaningful symbolism is a direct evolution of the inner vision of Bécquer, who in retrospect can be considered to be the first modern Spanish poet.

II *The 1920s and the Generation of 1927*

The poets beginning their careers around 1920 did so with an ever-increasing awareness of European currents in the arts. Salinas, a published poet since 1911, was a lecturer at the Sorbonne from 1914 to 1917, and Guillén from 1917 to 1923. Guillén began writing while in France where he met Paul Valéry, the master poet from the heritage of French symbolism. Valéry represented the ideal of "pure" poetry, an aesthetic concept that would receive considerable attention in Spain later in the decade. While Valéry's influence on the young writers has been exaggerated by some critics, he was certainly an inspiration to Guillén and Salinas because of his established position in European letters, just as Jiménez and Machado were the most highly esteemed poets in Spain.[2]

Not only were Spanish writers traveling abroad, but foreign ideas were being introduced into Spain as well. The talented Chilean poet Vicente Huidobro arrived in Madrid from Paris and expounded the literary novelty (to Spaniards) of *Ultraísmo* ("ultraism"), also known in Spain as *Creacionismo*. The creationist view of poetry was that its mission was to create a reality apart from nature, avoiding all imitation of the natural world. The principal contributions of creationism to Spanish poetry were an emphasis on metaphorical expression, and the introduction to the new generation of poets of a contemporary European literary current. There seems to be little influence of this movement in Guillén's work after some initial experimentation.[3]

In the parade of vanguardist literary "isms" that marched through Europe in the 1920s, surrealism is probably the best known because of the associations between it and Freudian psychoanalysis, which was becoming widely recognized at the time. An extension of ultraism, the surrealist ideal was to explore and describe a higher reality in the realm of the unconscious mind, hence the term surrealism itself, which means literally "above realism." Championed especially by André Breton in his *Manifeste surréaliste* [Surrealist Manifesto] in 1924, the movement found adherents but not committed converts in Spain, though García Lorca successfully exploited surrealist techniques in poetry and drama. Rafael Alberti and Vicente Aleixandre also experimented with surrealism, along with Salvador Dalí in painting and Luis Buñuel in cinema.

Spanish surrealism was not an extreme phenomenon. While some young writers did indeed search for a "higher reality" in art, there was little or no trancelike wandering through a dream world or affected "automatic writing" techniques. In an essay on his generation of writers, Guillén states succinctly and unequivocally his view of surrealism and the reaction of most of his contemporaries: "Without any dogmatic restrictions set by a school—there were neither school nor dogmas—these young men sought after a poetry that would be both art with all the severity of art and creation with all its genuine *élan*. An art of poetry, and therefore no mere effusion, neither in the manner of the last century nor as a violent, formless surge from the subconscious. There is no babble quite so empty as the subconscious left to its triviality. In Spain no one was ever satisfied with the surrealist 'document.' "[4]

The adherence to external reality, always a foundation of Guillén's poetry in particular, may be traced in part to the Spanish models of the young poets. Jiménez and especially Machado, though intensely attracted to the inner vision of the soul as they conceived it, never turned away from the outside world. Jiménez was probably the leading figure in Spanish poetry in the 1920s, and contemporary admiration for Machado was also profound, as Guillén once stated in an interview: "Antonio Machado es el primer poeta contemporáneo, la figura que más se agranda con los años" ("Machado is the leading contemporary poet, the figure whose stature increases with the years").[5]

A more lasting movement, perhaps better referred to as a poetic concept or stance, is the ideal of "pure" poetry that began to be noticed in the mid-1920s. Pure poetry was an attitude toward artistic creation rather than an "ism," representing a vital but disciplined collaboration of intuition and intellect. The intuitive aspect of pure poetry makes the attitude easier to describe than to define. The ideal was one of stripping away from the poetic text any elements irrelevant to the essence of the poetic experience for both the poet and reader. As Guillén stated concisely if perhaps facetiously in a now famous letter: "Poesía pura es todo lo que permanece en el poema después de haber eliminado todo lo que no es poesía" ("Pure poetry is all that remains in the poem after the elimination of all that is not poetry").[6] In particular, this meant removing as undesirable all overt sentimentality from the poem. Guillén describes the ideal more fully in an essay:

> Reality is depicted in the poem, but not described in its external *likeness*. Reality, not realism. And feeling, without which there is no poetry, has no need of gesticulation. Sentiment, not sentimentalism, which was damned by that group as the lowest of obscenities. This restraint in the displaying of emotions retains their vehemence, and indeed doubles their intensity. But for ears that hear not, harmonies such as these are almost confused with silence. That is why some of these poets were tried and found wanting for their coldness, even though they were dedicated to declaring their enthusiasm for the world, their fervor for life, their love for love.[7]

The mention of "coldness" alludes to a charge that plagued Guillén for a number of years, although critics during the last two decades have almost unanimously interred without ceremony what C. B.

Morris calls "the witless charge of coldness."[8] The now defunct accusation was the result of an exaggerated reaction to those who took seriously the ideal of pure poetry, particularly Guillén and Salinas. It is also worth noting that Guillén was his own severest critic during the 1920s. Many of his earliest poems underwent much revision in the author's quest for artistic perfection between their initial publication in journals and their reappearance in the first edition of *Cántico* (1928); others were left out altogether, discarded by the poet.[9] Ciplijauskaité points out that Salinas and especially Guillén may have taken to heart Valéry's notion that to become "classic," an author needs to carry within himself a critic, not a genius.[10]

The facile charge of coldness was made by a contemporary of Salinas and Guillén, Luis Cernuda, who called them "snobs,"[11] and later by Juan Ramón Jiménez, pursuant to a falling out with the group as a whole (about which more, below). Interestingly, another victim of an almost diametrically opposed but equally superficial critical judgment was García Lorca, an acutely sensitive and highly sophisticated artist characterized as "neo-popular" because of his use of folkloric material. Lorca reacted strongly to the label, and, in a letter written to Guillén in 1927, declared that the Gypsies were nothing but a literary theme, and complained that the attempt to associate him with Gypsy life made him seem to suffer from a "lack of education," and to appear "uncultured" and even "savage."[12] At any rate, although both these authors were the victims of sweeping generalizations, the reputations of both transcended them easily. In Guillén's case, the strict avoidance of all exaggeration and faddishness in *Cántico* led to the creation of a five-hundred-page book that may well prove to be of more permanent value than any other single poetic work written in Spain in this century.[13]

By the middle of the decade, the new generation of poets was in full bloom. Their works reflect such a degree of creativity and technical virtuosity that the group is generally considered to have begun producing in the 1920s the most vital and important Spanish poetry since the decline of the traditional Golden Age of Spanish literature in the seventeenth century. Curiously, however, the group did not react against the past, unlike the exponents of most European "isms" and the Spanish Generation of 1898. Dámaso Alonso, a member of Guillén's group who later devoted most of his attention to criticism, states that this was a generation of Spanish writers who rebelled against nothing.[14] Guillén, in fact, was writing sonnets during this period when hardly a poet in Europe or America would have used such an "antiquated" form.

Indicative of the poets' respect for the past was a gathering in Seville in December, 1927, to pay homage to the memory of Luis de Góngora, the Golden Age poet, on the tercentenary of his death. Góngora, a well-known but stylistically complex poet, had a reputation for linguistic obscurity and excessive baroque affectation. But the young poets saw in Góngora a consummate artist devoted to the creation of a purely literary language, and thus they recognized a kindred spirit in the quest for pure poetry. Góngora had little real influence on the writers, but he was venerated for representing what they also stood for, and so the meeting illustrates well the authors' concern with poetic theory. Guillén had written his doctoral dissertation on Góngora in 1924.

The meeting gave the Generation of 1927 its name, an arbitrary identification, arrived at because of a recognizable event that included playful as well as serious elements. Some of those in attendance declared themselves to be a "tribunal" and held a mock auto-da-fe ("act of faith") in the manner of the Spanish Inquisition with a ceremonial burning of books critical of Góngora. The pious tribunal "excommunicated" Guillén for not attending the book-burning. The entire event was financed by the bullfighter Ignacio Sánchez Mejías, who several years later died a bullfighter's death, memorialized in powerful elegies by Alberti and Lorca.[15]

A cause of considerable literary gossip in the 1930s was Juan Ramón Jiménez's gradual disenchantment with the poets who had revered him as their model a decade earlier. Jiménez had nurtured and encouraged the younger poets at the outset of their careers, and may have felt some disillusionment when, reaching their creative maturity, they began to drift away from his guidance. Whatever his reasons may have been, Jiménez's reactions were harsh. In a flattering note to Guillén in 1921, Jiménez writes: "Me complazco en felicitarle por lo que vengo leyendo de usted. . . . Todo esquisito [*sic*] y vivo,—carne y oro" ("I am happy to congratulate you for [your poetry] that I have been reading. Completely exquisite and alive—flesh and gold"). Twelve years later, the message becomes: "Quedan hoy retirados trabajo y amistad" ("Today work and friendship are withdrawn"). Jiménez remained bitter toward the younger poets years later, despite the fact that his own stellar career never suffered because of them in any way.[16]

The outbreak of the Spanish Civil War in 1936 caused the dispersal of the Generation. Although the year 1936 is catastrophically significant in Spanish history, it should not be inferred that the year signaled the end of the poets' importance in literature. Most left the country and continued their careers elsewhere in Europe, the United States, and Latin America. Their exile was shared by writers of other genres (the dramatist Alejandro Casona and the novelist Ramón Sender, for example), and by hundreds of thousands of their countrymen who could not, or would not, live in Spain under the dictatorship of Francisco Franco. The most tragic case was of course that of García Lorca. Near his home in the Granada area one month after the war began, he was summarily arrested and murdered by local Falangists.[17]

In summary, the movement which began so optimistically around 1920 was undone by political fanaticism and violence a decade and a half later. It is no surprise that the quality of writing dropped markedly in Spain after the war, the obvious reason being governmental censorship. The works of the poets continued to be published in other countries, but Spaniards living in Spain were often unable to read them.[18] In the years since Franco's death the climate has improved for free expression, and has seen the return of former exiles such as Guillén and Alberti.

Looking back on the literary production of the last half-century, it appears that those who speak cautiously of a second Golden Age in Spanish letters do so with reason. Present and future readers of poetry who agree with such a judgment will see the stirrings of a renaissance in the few dozen poems of Bécquer, a continued flowering in the introspective visions of Machado and Jiménez, and a culmination in the bright young men who met to honor Góngora in December of 1927.

III *The Life and Career of Jorge Guillén*

In addition to his life as a poet, Jorge Guillén has had a distinguished career as a university professor on three continents. Unlike some other members of the Generation of 1927, however, Guillén has not been associated with prominent historical incidents, and the salient facts of his biography can be summarized briefly.

The words that perhaps best characterize Guillén's life and career are "international" and "cosmopolitan"—this is the case in his upbringing and in his personal and professional life. Guillén was born in the old imperial city of Valladolid, where the most famous of Spanish monarchs, Ferdinand and Isabella, first met and were married in the fifteenth century. The father of the future poet, Julio Guillén Sáenz (1867–1950), was a businessman somewhat active in politics who also served on the administrative board of *El Norte de Castilla*, a Valladolid newspaper much respected in literary circles.[19]

Guillén's family was able to provide him with valuable educational opportunities that undoubtedly contributed to his cosmopolitan outlook. As a young man he studied in Switzerland. He received his university education in Madrid and Granada—while in Madrid, he lived for two years at the *Residencia de Estudiantes*, the well-known center of literary activities. After completing undergraduate degree requirements at the University of Granada, Guillén began traveling again, and in 1917 accepted a teaching position at the Sorbonne.

The years in Paris were extremely important for Guillén, in both his personal life and his career. While in France, he began to write and publish his first poems, and married a French woman, Germaine Cahen. Guillén later discarded some of his earliest poems as experiments, while others became the foundation of *Cántico*, the masterpiece that would take thirty years to construct. He returned to Spain as a professor during the crucial years of the Generation, leaving again to accept a position at Oxford.

Guillén returned to Spain and taught at the University of Seville from 1931 to 1938. He was in Spain when the Civil War broke out in 1936, and in September was arrested in Pamplona. It is unnerving to think that Guillén might easily have suffered the same insane fate as Lorca, in the year that the second edition of *Cántico* was published with a total of 125 poems. At any rate, he was released from custody and remained in Spain until 1938, when he left his homeland for exile in the United States.

Perhaps because of his international background, Guillén's exile was not the abysmal experience that it might well have been. Of course, there was the absence of his accustomed ambience and native language. In an interview, the poet once noted the negative aspects of exile, but added:

> En los Estados Unidos, donde fui muy bien acogido, mi exilio no ha sido desgraciado. Allí encontré la paz y la libertad. Además, el exilio no ha sido para mí un fenómeno radical, porque en cualquier punto de la tierra vuelvo a encontrar lo esencial: el aire, el agua, el sol, el hombre, la compañía humana.[20]

In the United States, where I was very well received, my exile has not been a misfortune. There I found peace and liberty. Furthermore, exile was not a radical experience for me, because at any point on the earth I find over and again what is essential: air, water, sun, man, human companionship.

Two years after arriving in America, Guillén accepted what would become his most permanent teaching position, at Wellesley College, where he was professor of Spanish for seventeen years. At Wellesley Guillén found the tranquillity to complete the 1945 and 1950 editions of *Cántico*. Also during this period, however, his wife Germaine died, to be remembered with powerful and touching nostalgia in *Que van a dar en la mar* [We Will End at the Sea], the second volume of *Clamor*.[21]

Guillén taught at several other universities in North and South America, and did not retire altogether from teaching until 1970, at the age of seventy-seven. During the 1950s he began to attract increasing attention as a poet of truly global significance, as can be seen from the number of prizes awarded to him since 1955.

In 1961, Guillén married a gracious Italian woman, Irene Mochi Sismondi. His home in the United States is in Cambridge, Massachusetts, although he has spent much time in Spain since the death of Franco (1975), and may not leave his native country again.[22]

The poet's lifelong international experience shows clearly in his work. In *Cántico* especially, but in the later work as well, events and scenes that Guillén recreates in poetry are removed from any anecdotal context that might limit the appeal or comprehensibility of a poem. So it is generally fruitless to ponder what Guillén might have been doing or thinking when he wrote any given poem, for each poem contains its own intrinsic meaning and message, and has a life apart from that of its creator. As the poet states simply: "El texto dice lo que él—por su propia cuenta—dice" ("the text says what is says of its own accord").[23] With this attitude in mind, the intent in the following chapter is to examine the salient themes of *Cántico* as they appear in the poetic texts themselves.

CHAPTER 2

Cántico: *The Poetry of Life*

"I was twenty-five when I began writing. Why had I never written before that? Because I never dared."[1] Jorge Guillén's earliest poems date from 1918, ten years before the appearance of *Cántico*, his first complete book of poetry. A slender volume of seventy-five poems, *Cántico* was published in 1928.[2] The calm but indefatigable affirmation of life that emerges from this collection was to characterize Guillén's poetry for more than two decades. The book has been aptly described by the American poet Archibald MacLeish: "Posterity, if it comes upon the great resounding Yes of *Cántico* among the tumbled fragments of our time, will not believe that No was all we had to answer to the world."[3]

If Guillén "never dared" to write poetry until a relatively mature age for a creative artist,[4] the coherence of vision and aesthetic purpose that often accompanies maturity is distinctly visible in *Cántico*. This unity is certainly related to the fact that the poet himself regarded the process of artistic creation with awe. Aesthetic expression is the medium through which the poet communicates his world view, so it is natural that the author should devote much attention to formulating his own theory of poetic creation.

The unity of thought that pervades *Cántico* has resulted in a somewhat unusual history of publication. Rather than issue a series of collections and later join them together as "complete poems," Guillén published four successively larger versions of *Cántico*, with new and occasionally revised poems in each edition of the work. The publication history is as follows: 1928, 75 poems; 1936, 125 poems; 1945, 270 poems; 1950, 334 poems. The 1928 edition of *Cántico* is divided into seven numbered sections. Since 1936, the poems have been grouped into five sections, each with its own subtitle.[5] However, the fundamental themes of the work are interwoven throughout the collection and transcend the separate sections. In 1945, Guillén added the significant subtitle *Fe de vida* [Testimony of Life] to the complete work. Since 1950, there have been two additional "editions" of *Cántico* (1962, 1973); these are reprints of the 1950 edition.

Naturally, the poet's thinking changed over the thirty years during which he created and published the four editions of *Cántico*. In addition to thematic evolution, individual poems often received minor revisions from one edition to another. Numerous examples of the poet's evolution can be seen in an excellent critical edition of the 1936 *Cántico* prepared by José Manuel Blecua. In Blecua's edition, all changes in these 125 poems are documented from their original appearance to their final form in *Our Air*.

In his attention to detail and style, Guillén is unmatched among his contemporaries.[6] Such preoccupation with the intricacies of form, coupled with a strict avoidance of romantic sentimentality, has led some critics to express the opinion that Guillén is "cold" or "dehumanized" in his poetry, despite his exuberant affirmation of many basic human values. The following judgment is typical of this critical attitude: "For most readers his song of joy in life is too abstractly conveyed. His agility and poetic concepts make him still a perfect but dehumanized poet."[7] As if to answer this kind of criticism, Guillén once commented in an interview:

> Jamás hemos pretendido que la poesía hubiese de ser sólo un ejercicio intelectual del que estuviese excluido el corazón. Esta es también la razón de que yo proteste con todas mis fuerzas contra la fórmula aconsejada por Ortega y Gasset: *deshumanización del arte*. La poesía como tal es forzosamente humana. ¿Cómo no habría de serlo? Quizás hayan existido la poesía inhumana o sobrehumana; pero un poema "deshumano" constituye una imposibilidad física y metafísica.[8]

> We have never claimed that poetry should be only an intellectual exercise with the heart excluded. This is [also] the reason that I vigorously protest the [aesthetic] formula suggested by Ortega y Gasset: *dehumanization of art*. Poetry is inescapably human. How could it be otherwise? Inhuman or superhuman poetry may have existed; but a "dehumanized" poem is a physical and metaphysical impossibility.

Since critical judgments depend upon the personal reactions of individual readers, it may be futile to debate the question of whether or not Guillén's poetry is stylistically sculptured and elaborated to the point of losing passion. It may also be the case that the intricacies of Guillén's style have discouraged an occasional literary critic.[9] On the other hand, the sensitive reader is more likely to appreciate the poet's attention to form and style, and be in agreement with Angel Valbuena Prat, who praises Guillén as "the classic of modern poetry."[10]

Cántico is a long book representing three decades of poetic creation. Its 334 poems range in length from four lines to thirteen pages. The intent in the present chapter is to describe and examine the salient themes of *Cántico* as they appear throughout the work in its definitive form. The thematic division is as follows: (1) the reality and primacy of the natural world, (2) the private, inner world of the individual, (3) eroticism, (4) time and death, (5) the symbolism of wholeness and fulfillment, (6) aesthetic theory—the function of poetry and the poet, and (7) the transition from *Cántico* to *Clamor*, Guillén's second major work.

The organic unity of *Cántico* is one of its more remarkable qualities, which is to say that any division or categorization is unavoidably arbitrary. The purpose in a thematic discussion is not to separate the work into distinct units, but to indicate the manner in which Guillén's hymnal to life is multifacted in scope and vision.

I *The Primacy of the World*

The consummate importance of the natural world in *Cántico* cannot be exaggerated. Guillén is a firm and enthusiastic believer in the intrinsic value of the objective world which surrounds him, repeatedly affirming its primacy and supremacy in relation to the position of humanity. There is nothing akin to Cartesian doubt expressed in *Cántico,* nor is there any manipulation or deformation of daily reality such as one finds in the surrealist experimentation of some of Guillén's contemporaries. Rather, the outside world in its ordinary reality is perceived to be of central significance for the individual and is therefore productive of faith in an absolute and concrete sense. Guillén's affirmation does not require cataclysmic circumstances for its expression, but is concentrated on the miracle of life in daily activity:

> Creo en la maravilla suficiente
> De esta calle a las once,
> Cuando la vida arrecia
> Con robustez normal, dichosa casi,

Humilde, realizada.[11]

I believe in the sufficient marvel
of this street at eleven,
when life rages
with normal vigor, almost fortunate,
humble, fulfilled.

The notable element in the above fragment is that the poet employs a quasi-religious tone which he applies to unremarkable and ordinary circumstances, although Guillén himself adheres to no specific religious doctrine. Faith in life is expressed with the phrases of a religious credo which is characteristic of Guillén's attitude toward daily reality. The "religious" aspect of the poem is especially apparent in the words "sufficient marvel." The phrase is reminiscent of the Roman Catholic theological concept of "sufficient grace," which in Catholic tradition is the grace given by God for purposes of salvation. Sufficient grace is the gift that God gives freely to each individual.[12] In Guillén's view of the world, it is reality itself that offers humanity a form of salvation in the self-realization of earthly life. The final poem of *Cántico* contains a similar quasi-religious declaration: "Yo soy merced a la hermosa / Revelación: este Globo" ("I am, by the grace of the beautiful / Revelation: this Globe," *AN*, 533).

Just as ordinary life is a "sufficient marvel," the world is given the status of a revelation in the above lines. By stating that the world *itself* is a revelation, the poet perceives the reality of the world and human life as having a certain divinity in and of themselves. Guillén elaborates on the significance of ordinary reality in an essay:

Ese ajuste entre los ojos y la luz, entre los pies y la tierra implica una coordinación tan obvia que a menudo los más atentos no la perciben. A sus oídos no llega esta armonía. Y, sin embargo, ninguna es superior a la de nuestro familiar equilibrio. Bien puede calificarse de maravilla.[13]

The relationship between the eyes and light, between the feet and earth implies a coordination so obvious that the most attentive observers often do not perceive it. And yet, there is no balance superior to our ordinary equilibrium. It can well be characterized as a marvel.

Elsewhere in the same essay, the poet makes an equally concise statement regarding his attention to daily reality: "*Cántico* atiende a esos instantes en que no sucede sino el fenómeno extraordinario de la normalidad" ("*Cántico* is devoted to those moments in which nothing transpires except the extraordinary phenomenon of normalcy").[14]

The primacy of the external world is succinctly described in the short poem "Fe" [Faith], in which Guillén also makes a metaphorical statement on the existential interaction that he perceives as existing between the world and the individual:

El alba. Todo me espera
También hoy.
Una fe con su certera
Voz de aliento
Me impulsa y mantiene fuera
De este mundo que yo soy,
En un viento
Que me enlaza a un real octubre.
No, no invento.
¿No soy yo quien él inventa?

(*AN*, 256)

Dawn. The whole awaits me
again today.
A faith with its unerring
voice of the spirit
keeps and impels me beside
this world that I am,
in a wind
that joins me to a real October.
No, I am not the inventor.
Does [all this] not discover me?

Frequently in Guillén's works, the title of a poem is indicative of the message to be conveyed. Here the anticipation accompanying the dawn inspires faith in the individual who affirms daily his own position in the world. This faith motivates the "believer" toward active participation in life. At the same time, one's faith is itself produced by the world as it is assimilated by the individual. The world is thus the source of both motivation and renewal: it attracts the believer, then continues to inspire his faith and his daily regeneration of spirit.

The importance given to nature is so great that Guillén insists on its primacy over his own existence in the final lines of the poem, in which he intentionally reverses the relationship of man and nature as it is ordinarily conceived. It should also be noted that the word "real" (line 7) has the double meaning of "real" and "royal" ("regal") in Spanish.

The fact that the natural world both attracts the individual and is assimilated by him ("this world that I am," line 6) implies a state of existential interaction between the poet and his surroundings. The outside world is important not only for what it *is*, but also for what it *represents*. This means that Guillén exalts the external world in part for its symbolic value. Throughout his works, Guillén employs as images objects from the environment, because through their natural qualities they represent in concrete form the internal feelings that the poet wishes to express. The symbolic object can therefore be defined as a link between the reality of the external world and the subjective—but equally "real"—dispositions of the individual. At all times in *Cántico* there is a vital relationship between symbol and psyche, the world and the mind. The word *symbol* itself derives from the Greek "to join," and that is Guillén's conception of the symbolic object—that is, his link with external reality. In "Abril de fresno" [April of the Ash], his reverence for reality is intensified by the noble appearance of the ash tree:

Una a una las hojas, recortándose nuevas,
Descubren a lo largo del abril de sus ramas
Delicia en creación. ¡Oh fresno, tú me elevas
Hacia la suma realidad, tú la proclamas!

(*AN*, 260)

One by one, the newly outlined leaves
discover the joy of creation in the April
of their branches. Ash, you raise me
to the supreme reality which you proclaim!

In this short poem, the double function of the tree is especially notable as it appears to the poet. The tree itself is viewed as an ideal summary of the reality which the speaker wishes to exalt—it is representative of springtime renewal in general, in addition to being a tree of particularly stately appearance. But the tree also "transcends" its natural position in the poet's view, because it joins him to the reality of the world beyond himself, thus helping him in his own quest for transcendence. Symbolically, therefore, the tree *is* the speaker, since it is his link to the world at the moment recorded in the poem.

In Guillén's view, the individual's interaction with the world occurs when the symbol—as intuited meaning—is perceived and assimilated. The symbol then joins one's inner profundity to external reality. It is therefore essential not only to *witness* empirical reality, but also to *absorb* it within oneself in the form of symbolic meaning. When the symbolic object is assimilated, the world is more than an intellectual scenario, for it becomes the embodiment of the poet's highest values and ideals. Guillén affirms the psychological internalization of the symbol in the following fragment from "Tiempo libre" [Free Time]:

Rico estoy
De tanta Creación atesorada.
Profundamente así me soy, me sé
Gracias a ti, que existes.
Me predispone todo sobre el prado
Para absorber la tarde.

(*AN*, 172)

I am rich
from so much treasured Creation.
I am profundly myself, I know myself
thanks to you, [world], who exist.
In the meadow, all this predisposes me
to absorb the afternoon.

These lines exemplify a marked tendency in Guillén's work to eliminate subject-object distinctions. The individual comes to know himself through the infinite world beyond him, in the form of objects that reflect his moods and dispositions. In the poet's words:

¿No merezco tal mañana?
Mi corazón se la gana.

Claridad, potencia suma:
Mi alma en ti se consuma.

(*AN*, 145)

Do I not deserve such a morning?
My heart will earn it.

Clarity, supreme power:
My soul consummates itself in you.

The aspects of the outside world that most notably attract the poet—its reality that produces faith in man, its attraction for and motivation of the individual, and its symbolic value—are brought together in "Más allá" [Beyond]. This is a crucially important poem for understanding Guillén's work in general, for here the poet affirms some ideas and attitudes that are essential both in *Cántico* and in the later work. "Beyond" is a long poem: fifty strophes of four lines each, with the poem divided into six sections. It was first included in the 1936 *Cántico,*[15] and appears as the initial poem in the 1945 and 1950 editions. Guillén's placement of the poem indicates that he intends it to be his basic declaration of principles, and it indeed contains several dominant themes of *Cántico,* especially concerning the relationship that exists between the individual and his surroundings, and the existential bond that Guillén perceives as joining the two.

The rest of this section on the primacy of the world in *Cántico* is devoted to a consideration of the ideas expressed in "Beyond." The title is a general reference to the world at large that lies beyond the speaker and awaits him as a new day dawns. As is frequently the case in *Cántico,* the poet describes an ordinary situation in which he sees profound and vital meaning. The length of this important work precludes its presentation in complete form, so the poem is somewhat abridged in an attempt to relate it to the points raised in this chapter. Roman numerals indicate Guillén's division of the poem into sections; other divisions are intended to facilitate a thematic discussion of the poet's salient ideas in the work:

I

(El alma vuelve al cuerpo,
Se dirige a los ojos
Y choca.)—¡Luz! Me invade
Todo mi ser. ¡Asombro!

Intacto aún, enorme,
Rodea el tiempo. Ruidos
Irrumpen. ¡Cómo saltan
Sobre los amarillos

Todavía no agudos
De un sol hecho ternura
De rayo alboreado
Para estancia difusa,

Mientras van presentándose
Todas las consistencias
Que al disponerse en cosas
Me limitan, me centran!

. . . .

(*AN*, 26)

I

(The soul returns to the body,
arrives at my eyes
with a shock.)—Light! It floods
my being with wonder.

Time, immense and untouched,
surrounds me. Noises break forth:
they spring lightly,
over the dull

yellow hues
of the soft sunlight
of dawn
in this diffused room,

while all the substances
gradually appear which
limit and center me,
as they become things.

The poem begins with a description of the dawn as its first manifestations become visible to the poet. Guillén sees his personal situation as analogous to the natural world: the appearance of light corresponds to his own return to waking consciousness. The joy characteristic of Guillén's poetry is expressed in the first strophe of *Cántico,* almost as a preview of the work as a whole. In the second strophe, the speaker relates his enthusiasm at the thought of discovering the new day that awaits him ("time surrounds me"), then mentions the sounds and colors of the morning that fill his room and his imagination.

A subtle change of thought is introduced in the fourth strophe, as the speaker's attention moves from scenography to poetic commentary. The appearance of *things*—concrete realities—provides the external context that he needs in order to delineate his own position in the world. The image of things that "limit and center" the poet is therefore to be understood positively and affirmatively. The poet is able to establish his own position in the world thanks to the perspective of external reality. This indicates that the title of the poem, "Beyond," does not imply a dichotomy between subject (poet) and object (world), but instead stresses the relationship that binds them.

In the following strophes, the speaker moves from the implications of primarily *spatial* relationships to his position in the *temporal* flow:

> Todo está concentrado
> Por siglos de raíz
> Dentro de este momento,
> Eterno y para mí.
>
> Y sobre los instantes
> Que pasan de continuo
> Voy salvando el presente,
> Eternidad en vilo.
> . . . .
>
> (*AN*, 27)

> Rooted in the centuries,
> time culminates
> in this very moment,
> eternal and mine.
>
> And from the endless stream
> of passing moments
> I save the present,
> a visible eternity.

The theme of time pervades *Cántico,* and will be separately considered in section 4 of this chapter. In "Beyond," Guillén concentrates on the culmination of time in the arrival of the present moment. That is to say that the process of creation is complete—and therefore fulfilled—at the moment described. This declaration includes an implicit rejection of any "systematic" view of time that would indicate a culmination at some future moment and render the present meaningless. He prefers to concentrate on the fullness of the present and its preservation in poetry.

By asserting that the present is to be "saved," Guillén enters the scene in his role as *poet* in addition to participant.[16] Here he expresses a thought similar to the traditional notion—Horace's *exegi monumentum*—that the artist immortalizes a moment or event in his work. The present is captured and preserved, and thus escapes temporal oblivion. While Guillén does not dwell on this aspect of his presence, he does take note of his function as poetic commentator as well as witness. (Guillén's view of the poet and his function is studied specifically in section 6 of this chapter.)

After declaring his estimation of the importance of the present, Guillén shifts his emphasis to the basic affirmation of this poem in particular and *Cántico* in general: his exuberant exclamation of joy in life, in his own being and normalcy. The expression of happiness found in these lines summarizes well the poet's attitude toward life as he records it in *Cántico:*

Corre la sangre, corre
Con fatal avidez.
A ciegas acumulo
Destino: quiero ser.

Ser, nada más. Y basta.
Es la absoluta dicha.
¡Con la esencia en silencio
Tanto se identifica!
. . . .

(*AN*, 27)

My blood flows
with fateful eagerness.
I blindly assemble my destiny
in my desire to be.

Being, nothing more, is sufficient.
It is absolute joy.
It becomes essence,
silently.

The affirmation of these verses can best be understood and appreciated if the lines are considered as representative of Guillén's outlook as a whole. The declaration that being *itself* is sufficient self-realization in life—that it is "absolute joy"—may seem simple enough at first reading. The lines become more meaningful, however, if one reflects briefly on the plethora of contemporary literature that is basically *negative* in its orientation. Guillén's fundamental optimism becomes more remarkable when one considers its singularity within the context of twentieth-century art; this is the point that Archibald MacLeish makes well in the paragraph quoted earlier.

The second strophe also has special significance within the historical context of Spanish literature. As mentioned in the preceding chapter, the outstanding Spanish poet of the nineteenth century is Gustavo Adolfo Bécquer (1836–1870), whose fame is based primarily on a slender volume of posthumously published verse. The poems that comprise Bécquer's *Rimas* [Poems] constitute the most intense and profound expressions of Spanish romanticism. Bécquer is "typically" romantic in his embracing of high ideals and consequent dissatisfaction with his daily circumstances. One of his better-known poems contains a list of natural beauties and daily pleasures, then concludes with his personal exclamation of lament: "¡Y qué desgracia que esto solo no baste!"[17] ("And what a pity that this should not be enough!") Guillén's lines appear to be a direct response to Bécquer's famous cry of disillusionment and pessimistic idealism. Writing more than half a century later, Guillén considers the same idea of daily life in all its normalcy and affirms, in effect, "yes, it is enough." Given Guillén's erudition and career as a professor of literature, it seems safe to conclude that his seeming response to Bécquer is an intentional commentary.

One possible reason for Guillén's appreciation of daily life has been suggested: that is his acute perception of the symbolic value of ordinary reality. Objects of the environment are esteemed since they lead to the discovery of the essences that they represent. This essence is affirmed in the above two strophes, since it is reached through the "sufficient marvel" of the ambience.

The first section of this long poem ends with another expression of Guillén's relation to the world in his role as poet. In addition to realizing his need for the world, he is aware of the reciprocity of the relationship as he affirms his own contributions. Here he speaks of his immediate surroundings as they become clearer in the light of dawn that enters his room:

> Todo me comunica,
> Vencedor, hecho mundo,

Su brío para ser
De veras real, en triunfo.

Soy, más, estoy. Respiro.
Lo profundo es el aire.
La realidad me inventa,
Soy su leyenda. ¡Salve!

(*AN*, 28)

All the world shares with me
— a conqueror—
its determination
to be triumphantly real.

I am, and more: I am here and now.
I breathe in the profundity of the air.
Reality creates me—welcome!—
I am its legend.

The objects of the room come into focus, and the poet turns his thoughts to his aesthetic relationship with the world. Here it is essential to distinguish between the speaker's personal need for the world, and his use of it for the purpose of poetic creation. The two views are closely related, and yet there is a notable difference of attitude between one type of attentiveness and the other. In the first instance, the speaker reacts to his surroundings as a sensitive observer who sees in the ambience a symbolic reflection of himself. This attitude is indicative of a responsive awareness, but of course it is not in itself aesthetic, regardless of its importance for the individual.

The second, aesthetic, view of reality derives from the first and transcends it. Here the poet not only perceives and appreciates the environment, he exploits it for eventual recreation in poetry, thereby manipulating the world in his own way, as he selectively adapts it to his work. Aesthetic manipulation by the artist makes him a "conqueror," Guillén states in the first strophe. It is notable in this strophe that the speaker continues to affirm the reality of the world—this external reality does not diminish in value when exploited by the poet, and thus it remains "triumphantly real."

The second strophe contains brief mention of yet another aesthetic notion. Guillén reaffirms the quality of immediacy in his contact with the surroundings ("here and now"), and also the mutual participation between the poet and nature ("reality finds me"). After stating that reality creates him, the poet adds in conclusion that he is its "legend." Within the context of the poem, Guillén is apparently using the word "legend" to mean "inscription" or "reading." Thus, he makes a metaphorical statement on his literal function as a poet: to comment on the world in verse. The poetic recreation of nature results in conscious clarity where it was previously lacking, and the poet makes a contribution to the world that he exploited as a "conqueror." Of course, the notion of conscious clarity resulting from artistic creation is ancient. In modern Europe, the idea was espoused by Nietzsche, whose thought was widely influential in Spain at the end of the nineteenth century and into the twentieth. Among Guillén's contemporaries, conscious clarity through art is a notable theme in the late work of Pedro Salinas.[18]

Sections 2, 3, and 4 of the poem deal with various aspects of physical objects and the necessity of their reality for the poet. In section 5, Guillén addresses himself to what the objects mean for the individual who is sensitive to them and to their possible symbolic meaning:

> Por aquella pared,
> Bajo un sol que derrama,
> Dora y sombrea claros
> Caldeados, la calma
>
> Soleada varía.
> Sonreído va el sol
> Por la pared. ¡Gozosa
> Materia en relación!
>
> Y mientras, lo más alto
> De un árbol—hoja a hoja
> Soleándose, dándose,
> Todo actual—me enamora.
>
> Errante en el verdor
> Un aroma presiento,
> Que me regalará
> Su calidad: lo ajeno,
>
> Lo tan ajeno que es
> Allá en sí mismo. Dádiva

De un mundo irremplazable:
Voy por él a mi alma.

(*AN*, 32)

The sunlit calm varies
along the wall,
beneath a sun which
gilds, shades and spreads

warmth across
the room, smilingly.
Joyful matter
in relation!

And a treetop
inspires love in me,
giving itself fully,
leaf by leaf, in the sun.

In the verdure I sense
a wandering fragrance
which will give me
its own superior quality: otherness,

otherness that is
there, in and of itself. It is the gift
of an irreplaceable world
that leads me to my soul.

The two initial strophes of the section contain a repetition of the characterization of the room as the sun illuminates it; the description is similar to that of section 1 (strophes 3 and 4). An interesting difference is that in the present strophes, Guillén states that the sun *itself* moves across the room and spreads warmth. This metaphorical image stresses the lack of categorical separation, in the poet's mind, between his own life and the world beyond him. The thought is emphasized in the final sentence of strophe 2: "Joyful matter / in relation!" The absence of categorical distinctions seen in these lines is reminiscent of the attitude expressed in "April of the Ash" and "Free Time," studied earlier in this chapter.

In the third strophe, the poet reiterates another idea mentioned previously—the notion that the symbolic meaning of nature can lead to an increased awareness of one's inner self, as the individual's dispositions are reflected or represented externally in the world. As Guillén states in "Free Time": "I am profoundly myself, I know myself / thanks to you, [world], who exist."

The fourth strophe is a reaffirmation of the primacy of the world in Guillén's poetry. The speaker insists on the necessity of the outside world, which assists him in the completion of his own being. Guillén goes on to state that his personal need for the world does not mean that it has importance only as an extension of his own imagination or will. Nature has its own independence: it is a "gift" to humanity, but can get along well without us. The last line of the section repeats the theme of self-discovery and completion with the symbolic assistance of nature.

In the concluding section of the poem, Guillén extends the attitudes and sentiments expressed in part 1. In the initial section, the poet describes the gradual arrival of dawn which parallels his own return to waking consciousness. He declares that the surrounding objects are necessary for him, as they "limit and center" him in the world, and affirms the value of the present moment, declaring his own joy in being. The first section concludes with two strophes in which the speaker comments on the function of the poet.

In section 6, Guillén unites the different themes of this long poem—that is, he returns to the affirmations of section 1, in light of the thoughts that appear in the intervening five sections. As he concludes the poem, Guillén concentrates on the effect that external harmony has upon him as he assimilates within himself the beauty that surrounds him:

> ¡Oh perfección! Dependo
> Del total más allá,
> Dependo de las cosas.
> . . . .
>
> Dependo en alegría
> De un cristal de balcón,
> De ese lustre que ofrece
> Lo ansiado a su raptor,
>
> Y es de veras atmósfera
> Diáfana de mañana,
> Un alero, tejados,
> Nubes allí, distancias.
> . . . .

Nunca separa el cielo.
Ese cielo de ahora
—Aire que yo respiro—
De planeta me colma.

¿Dónde extraviarse, dónde?
Mi centro es este punto:
Cualquiera. ¡Tan plenario
Siempre me aguarda el mundo!
. . . .

(*AN*, 33–34)

Perfection! I depend
on the totality of the beyond,
I am sustained by things.

Joyfully, I depend
on a balcony window,
and on the lustrous sunlight
which offers to me—its abductor—my wish:

the crystal air
of morning,
the ceiling, rooftops,
the distant clouds.

The sky is never apart.
At this moment the sky
—the air that I breathe—
fills me with a sense of the planet.

Where can one go astray?
This place—or any other—
is my center. The world,
so complete, forever awaits me.

In this fragment, particularly in the final two strophes, Guillén speaks metaphorically of the "internalization" of the outside world as he "absorbs" reality within himself. Since the world provides him with an outside perspective on his own life, with its help he is able to establish his own "limit" and "center." His "center" is thus a psychological realization of his place in the world—the exploration of the ambience is a way of coming to know himself. Self-knowledge is the reason the poet can state that his "center" can be found anywhere. His perspective on the world is applied to himself, and he finds self-realization regardless of the specific surroundings. The poet is expressing an attitude, as opposed to, or in addition to, a literal description.

The poem concludes with another comment on the light of dawn and its meaning for the individual. The theme of time is again used here. In these final strophes, Guillén reaffirms his estimation of the present moment, and also turns his attention to the idea that creation—the universe as he perceives it—begins anew with the dawn of a new day:

Es la luz del primer
Vergel, y aun fulge aquí,
Ante mi faz, sobre esa
Flor, en ese jardín.

Y con un empuje henchido
De afluencias amantes
Se ahinca en el sagrado
Presente perdurable

Toda la creación,
Que al despertarse un hombre
Lanza la soledad
A un tumulto de acordes.

(*AN*, 35)

This is the primordial
light which shines even here,
before my face, on that
flower, in the garden.

And with a thrust filled
with a loving flow,
all of creation
hastens in the sacred,

eternal present,
this creation which,
as a man awakens,
hurls his solitude
toward a commotion of harmony.

The first mention of time in the poem, in section 1, concentrates on the fullness of the present moment, and on the idea that the present is saved from oblivion in the work of the poet. In the above concluding strophes, Guillén adds another perspective on the concept of the temporal march. Here he sees the dawn as futurity, the promise of life to come as a new day begins. Creation is reborn in a daily renewal. The light which the speaker perceives is therefore "primordial," since it is the first light of creation in its daily manifestation. The present is "eternal" in the poet's view, but it is also the future as the world renews itself.

In the final lines of the poem, Guillén repeats his feeling that the basic attitude of man in the world should be one of participation in the ambience. Ultimately, primacy in life is not found in the subject (the individual) or the object (the world), but in the interaction of the two. The aspect of this vision that is especially notable in Guillén's work is the transcendence of egocentricity in his world view. He does not turn away from the world in order to explore his own being, but finds himself through an existential dialogue with reality.

As stated at the beginning of this analysis, "Beyond" is a critically important work which sets the tone for much of *Cántico*. A brief review of the themes of this poem will therefore also summarize much of what Guillén affirms throughout *Cántico* concerning the importance of reality. He considers the dawn to be analogous to the arrival of waking consciousness in the individual. Early in the poem, he insists on the importance of things—realities—which provide him with a needed perspective on the world; this is the principal theme of the poem, to which he returns repeatedly. Other salient ideas include Guillén's comments on various aspects of time, and the poet's view of his own function in time and nature. But the single most important idea here is the *dialogue with reality* that enables the individual to discover and to complete himself as he discovers the world around him. Thus it is that physical things "limit and center" the speaker (section 1), lead him to his soul (section 5), and sustain him in life (section 6).

The importance of reality in "Beyond" parallels Guillén's view of the world in numerous other poems. In this discussion of reality as it is perceived and characterized in *Cántico,* the main ideas are the supreme faith in the world that instills feelings akin to religiosity in the poet, and the attraction and motivation that the world provides. It has been suggested that one reason for the affirmative view of the world is Guillén's appreciation for the vision and understanding that the world gives him regarding his own being—the world is supremely important for itself and for its symbolic value—hence the absolute necessity of the dialogue with reality.

The foregoing discussion of reality has centered on the importance of the world, and on the interaction between the world and the individual. In the following section, the intent is to examine Guillén's thoughts when he turns his attention inward, explores the private world of the mind, and penetrates the inner recesses of his being.

II *The World of the Mind*

In few works of any national literature or historical period is the balance between the world and the mind so remarkably consistent as it is in Guillén's *Cántico*. While the poet insists on the primacy of objective reality in relation to the individual, it can be said that, in *Cántico*, the poet alternates between an outward vision and one which is directed inward. Another manner of stating the apparent dichotomy is to say that Guillén often seems to write poetry which can be characterized as either "extroverted" or "introverted" in terms of subject matter.[19] However, it is necessary to add that the dichotomy is indeed only apparent, because Guillén normally observes and maintains a clear equilibrium that precludes extremes.

The poems chosen for analysis in this section illustrate the thematic balance of *Cántico*. For purposes of discussion, the poems are divided into three groups: two poems characterizing or describing inner thoughts with strictly external metaphors, a poem in which the speaker expresses his own private thoughts in terms of the world, and last, a sonnet in which Guillén implies that sleep is the most fundamental form of introspection, since the concerns of the world do not penetrate the psychic drama of the solitary dreamer.

Guillén finds it natural to express introverted dispositions in poems which contain metaphors drawn from the outside world. While such poems are often intimate and autobiographical in nature, the poet still looks to the ambience for symbols that reflect his inner feelings. Even in his introspective moments, therefore, Guillén formulates his thoughts using images which concretely embody those sentiments that he wishes to express.

The poet's declaration of his inner thoughts using external metaphors is not surprising if one bears in mind Guillén's estimation of the natural world. The world itself is our ultimate treasure, both for what it is and what it represents. In the poet's words: "Creo en la Creación más evidente" ("I believe in the most evident Creation," *AN*, 283). Thus it is that in a poem such as "Beyond," Guillén's description of the arrival of daylight also applies to his own consciousness. The following short poem, "¿Ocaso?" [Sunset?], is typical of Guillén's tendency to express introspection with external images:

> Íntima y dúctil, la sombra aguardando aparece
> Sobre las piedras y sobre las brañas. Lo oscuro
> Se junta. ¿Fin? El silencio recibe en su alfombra
> Los sones menguantes del mundo. Pozo de ocaso,
> Nada se pierde. La tierra en su ser profundiza.
>
> (*AN*, 328)

> Intimate and compliant, the waiting shadows appear
> over the rocks and summer pastures. The darkness
> gathers. The end? A carpet of silence absorbs
> the diminishing sounds of the world. Nothing is lost
> in the well of darkness. The earth plunges into its being.

The title of the poem appears as a rhetorical question, in itself a commentary on the lines that follow. The Spanish word "ocaso" has the same double meaning as "sunset" in English: the word frequently refers to any "ending" in the figurative sense. Guillén therefore poses the question of whether the sunset brings with it a finality beyond the physical absence of light and those activities normally associated with daylight and the waking hours in general. Another reference to "Beyond" may serve to illustrate this point. The speaker in "Beyond" stresses the attraction by the world that accompanies the arrival of daylight. In the present poem, the implication is that nothing is lost at sunset, but that different activities are pursued. The poet's rhetorical question, then, provides an indirect comment on the idea that the physical phenomenon of the sunset is in no way an "end" to intellectual or spiritual pursuits of interest.

The poem itself is presented in two parts: the speaker describes the scene, then comments. Guillén's economy of expression is especially apparent in this poem. In few words, the poet creates an ambience of tranquillity and peace which fittingly accompanies the enveloping darkness. He asks—rhetorically—if the end of the day brings with it a more general finality. The concluding two sentences of the poem provide an answer that is stylistically understated but conceptually emphatic. Here the poet states, in effect, that darkness is conducive to introspection, as opposed to the outwardly directed activities of the day.

Guillén's thought is perhaps clarified by a related idea, the Oriental concept of *yang* and *yin,* masculine and feminine principles representing the active and passive modes of being in human life and in the world in general. One writer on the subject describes the *yang* as "active . . . bright . . . positive," and the *yin* as "dark . . . mysterious, secret."[20] The Taoist concept parallels Guillén's poetic commentary on the intimate and internally directed pensiveness associated with the night, which complements or balances the outside pursuits of the workaday world.

It should be noted that the poet makes no value judgment regarding the relative merit of one orientation or the other. The lack of an expressed preference is indicative of the balance found throughout *Cántico*. Life is enthusiastically accepted and pursued in all its facets. Therefore, the introspection of nighttime is not valued more or less than the goals of day. This trait indicates not vacillation, but equilibrium. The *yang* and *yin* are applicable to Guillén's thought insofar as he cultivates and affirms the necessity of achieving and maintaining balance in all areas of life.

Guillén's metaphorical expression is also notable. As stated earlier, the poet varies in his degree of *personal* involvement in the idea or sentiment treated in a particular poem. In "Sunset?," Guillén describes and affirms the specifically human phenomenon of introspection. And yet, there is no mention of human beings in the poem. Rather, the fundamental idea of the poem is projected symbolically onto the natural world, making the thought less personal (Jorge Guillén's) and more universal (poetry). While the speaker does not enter into the poem personally, he allows the reader to participate by arriving at his own conclusions with respect to the general validity of the message.

Guillén makes a similar point regarding introspection via another metaphor, the tree, a symbolic representation of human life and activity. The tree is an ideal symbol of human aspirations and profundity. While the upper branches reach toward heaven and light, the tree depends equally on its roots which penetrate the subterranean darkness. The tree is therefore a natural symbol of the human condition, and Guillén is not at all unique in employing it as an image.[21] In "April of the Ash," seen in the previous section, the "upward" aspect of the tree is emphasized, as is the manner in which the tree attracts the poet to reality in both a literal and a symbolic sense. In the present examination of Guillén's introspective poetry, it will be profitable to analyze another poem in which a tree appears as the central image. In "Árbol del otoño" [Tree in Autumn], the poet elaborates the metaphor of a tree with an inner vitality crucial to its life, albeit invisible to the world at large. The speaker begins with a simple, ordinary observation, then proceeds to a more general application:

> Ya madura
> La hoja para su tranquila caída justa,
>
> Cae. Cae
> Dentro del cielo, verdor perenne, del estanque.
>
> En reposo,
> Molicie de lo último, se ensimisma el otoño.
>
> Dulcemente
> A la pureza de lo frío la hoja cede.
>
> Agua abajo,
> Con follaje incesante busca a su dios el árbol.
>
> (*AN*, 306)

> Mature now,
> the leaf falls to its just and tranquil
>
> end. It falls
> into the sky of the pond, the enduring verdure.
>
> Restfully,
> in final softness, autumn becomes absorbed into itself.
>
> The leaf
> yields sweetly to the purity of the cold.
>
> The tree,
> with water below, seeks its god with incessant foliage.[22]

It is important to note the conceptual similarity between this poem and "Sunset?" The previous poem contains an implicit comparison between day and night, with darkness esteemed as conducive to introspection—"the earth plunges into its being." In "Tree in Autumn," the comparison involves the seasonal cycle. Guillén, in general, considers spring and summer the seasons for outgoing activities, while fall and winter appear to be more appropriate for private, meditative pursuits. The two poems therefore convey similar messages, although the images employed are distinct.

The specific images of "Tree in Autumn" require some additional commentary. The cyclical nature of life as it appears in the poem is clear enough (Guillén's reference to the "just" fall of the leaf involves his feelings about time and death, as will be discussed in section 4 of this chapter). The internal equilibrium of the poem begins to emerge in the second strophe. Here, the poet establishes a balanced opposition as he mentions the reflection of the sky in the pond. Furthermore, the greenness of the pond indicates a continuing manifestation of life which is not subject to the same natural laws governing the cycle of the tree—the leaf dies, but falls into the pond which is a distinct and ongoing microcosm of life.

In the third strophe, the poet moves to the human application of his observation. He asserts that the autumn season becomes absorbed in its own being—perhaps "withdrawn" or "introverted" in terms of human disposition or experience. This declaration parallels the affirmation of "Sunset?" that the earth plumbs its own depths in the darkness. The fourth strophe returns the reader's attention to the scene of the poem, so that the initial observation is not forgotten after the introduction of the second thematic element, that of withdrawal.

The concluding sentence of the poem metaphorically restates the theme of introspection. Here again, the poet depends on a natural phenomenon for a metaphysical conclusion, for the reader is certainly well aware that the tree does not literally "die" in autumn, but that its life is maintained away from view in the subterranean roots. The tree remains alive—"with incessant foliage"—but it is "absorbed" in itself, as dictated by the laws of the season.

In both "Sunset?" and "Tree in Autumn," then, Guillén comments on a human situation by employing symbolic images drawn from nature. People do not appear in the poems, not even the speaker. In the following poem, "Rama del otoño" [Autumn Branch], the poet enters personally. His concern is again introspection, and he comments especially on the vitality of active imagination (this poem appears immediately after "Tree in Autumn" in *Cántico*):

Cruje otoño.
Las laderas de sombras se derrumban en torno.

Arbol ágil,
Mundo terso, mente monda, guante en mano al aire.

¡Cómo aguzan
Su pormenor tranquilo las nuevas nervaduras!

Chimenea:
Exáltame en resumen lejanías de sierras.

. . . Sí, se enarca,
Extremo estío, la orografía de la brasa.

(*AN*, 306–7)

Autumn crackles.
The shadowy slopes tumble all around.

A lively tree,
a brilliant world, a clear mind, a gloved hand to the air.

How much sharper
the leaf ribbings become in their serene detail!

Fireplace:
exalt for me—in summary—the distant mountains.

. . . Yes, as in extreme summer,
the orography of the embers arches upward.

The entire poem constitutes an extraordinarily elaborate metaphor, in which the speaker relates his imaginative reaction while watching a log or branch burn in a fireplace. In the first strophe, he describes the log as if it were a mountain or hillside, and the changing shadows are those cast by the flames. Thus the active imagination of the poet is expressed immediately. At the same time, he establishes a perceived relationship between the outside world (autumn) and the mind's eye. Another way of stating the idea is to say that Guillén sees the macrocosm of the world in terms of the microcosm of the fireplace, as he intellectually and poetically reduces the world to the proportions of the fireplace.

The poet's mental "reduction" of the macrocosm is especially evident in the fourth strophe. Here the speaker, utilizing a somewhat unusual stylistic technique, addresses the fireplace directly, and commands a "summary" of the mountains in the distance. In the final lines, he turns his attention to the log itself, and completes the metaphor of the mountain begun in the first strophe. "Orography" is that branch of geology which deals with the formation and variations of mountains. The reference in the poem, then, is apparently to the uneven ridges of flame and bark along the top of the burning log, hence the embers in the fireplace and their metaphorical "orography."

Within the context of the topic of discussion—introspection and imagination—it is important to note that the poet refers to the world beyond him without directing his attention away from the fireplace, recreating the world internally with his own thoughts, and perceiving great distances within the confines of a single room. This manifestation of a vivid imagination underscores the intellectual and emotional equilibrium so characteristic of Guillén's poetry. The first poem of *Cántico*, "Beyond," is an invitation to enter the world. In "Autumn Branch," the poet remains indoors, but brings the world in with him. As Guillén states in another short poem concerned with the intimate and introspective quality of winter: "Cerré las puertas. El mundo me ciñe" ("I closed the doors. The world surrounds me," *AN*, 332).

The poems chosen for analysis thus far in this section portray the life of the mind with images that project the poet's thought onto the ambience. Occasionally, however, introspection becomes private to the point that the outside world is temporarily bracketed out of the poet's thoughts. Such a situation is relatively infrequent in the work of a poet whose estimation of external reality is paramount, but does occur when the poet becomes engrossed in meditative contemplation. Guillén feels that the dream vision of sleep is an immersion in the depths of one's own being. While he never doubts the value of experience in the outside world, he also affirms the validity of *psychic* truth perceived in the dream. His attitude toward sleep and dreaming is essentially in accord with the view of some modern psychologists, notably C. G. Jung, that dreams are a necessary manifestation of the unconscious mind in the psychology of the individual. The following sonnet, "Cierro los ojos" [I Close

My Eyes], offers a declaration of Guillén's positive attitude toward the existential validity of the dream. The poem is prefaced by an epigraph from the French poet Stéphane Mallarmé, "une rose dans les ténèbres" ("a rose in the darkness"):

Cierro los ojos y el negror me advierte
Que no es negror, y alumbra unos destellos
Para darme a entender que sí son ellos
El fondo en algazara de la suerte,

Incógnita nocturna ya tan fuerte
Que consigue ante mí romper sus sellos
Y sacar del abismo los más bellos
Resplandores hostiles a la muerte.

Cierro los ojos. Y persiste un mundo
Grande que me deslumbra así, vacío
De su profundidad tumultuosa.

Mi certidumbre en la tiniebla fundo,
Tenebroso el relámpago es más mío,
En lo negro se yergue hasta una rosa.

(*AN*, 290)

I close my eyes, and the blackness shows me
that it is not blackness, and illuminates bright rays
which lead me to understand them as
the noisy depths of fate,

a nocturnal mystery which is so strong now
that it breaks its seal before me
and extracts radiant brilliances
—opposed to death—from the abyss.

I close my eyes. And a great world
persists and bewilders me,
emptied of its tumultuous depths.

I establish my certainty in the darkness,
the dark flash of lightning is mine,
[and] a rose rises up in the blackness.

The symbolic meaning of this poem is related to that of "Tree in Autumn," discussed above. In the previous poem, a tree is described as becoming absorbed into itself and finding its inner transcendence, its "god," away from public view in the subterranean roots. Introspection is thus affirmed with imagery drawn from the outside world. In "I Close My Eyes," the attitude of the poet is essentially unchanged, but the description here is much more intimate and personal. The positive attitude of the speaker is immediately evident. The apparent contradiction of the first strophe—personal illumination in darkness—shows that the poet is sensitive to the internal enlightenment emanating from the depths of his own being. The various descriptive words indicating inner light point to the ideal of internally generated inspiration and guidance, which is simply to say that the poet finds inspiration within himself as well as in the world.

It is probably intentional that sleep—or dreaming—is not mentioned as such, although implied by the phrase "nocturnal mystery." The reader is thus left with the impression that either sleep *or* deep introspection can lead to illumination from within. The idea of the dream vision becomes a metaphor describing inner contemplation or meditation. The inner vision is unclear in logical terms—indeed, it is frequently baffling to the intellect—but Guillén affirms that it provides a form of intuited contact with his own roots that penetrate the inner recesses of the psyche. The human paradox of inner understanding which results from inner darkness can be seen in the opposed but complementary thoughts of the last two strophes: bewilderment leads to certainty, and darkness to light. These oppositions are resolved in the image of the rose, a traditional symbol of totality and perfection.

The poems discussed above are characteristic of the manner in which Guillén describes introspection and affirms its necessity in human life. This is certainly natural when one reflects on the balanced view of life that typifies *Cántico*. Just as there is a "beyond" *(más allá)*, so there is a "within" *(más acá,)* awaiting exploration. And so it appears that the speaker is engaged in *self*-discovery, whether his attention is focused inward or on the outside world. His dialogue can transpire with objective reality, or with himself, and either external or internal contact leads to increased knowledge of one's essence.

A consideration of introspection in Guillén's poetry should not exaggerate the poet's own view of its importance. While Guillén firmly believes in self-examination, he is not an introverted poet in his basic outlook. The world beyond him is always seen as infinitely superior to the individual, too much so to ignore it in favor of his own thoughts: the world situates him, and without it he is nothing. And yet, the world is supremely important, in part because the individual views it as an external, symbolic projection of himself. He therefore finds his essence in the world beyond, as he does in the world within. The world and the mind represent two complementary and intertwined paths to self-realization. But the poet also devotes much attention and feeling to another, more fulfilling, method of reaching the soul and the emotions: that of human relatedness and love.

III *Eroticism*

Cántico is a love poem. In this regard, it is useful to recall the complete title of the work: *Canticle: Testimony of Life*. Guillén's testimony to living is in a effect a monumental hymnal of praise. It is therefore difficult to examine a crucial theme such as love as a separate or independent topic in *Cántico,* since the idea of love is found almost literally on every page of the work. The central position of love has been noted by critics. Willis Barnstone writes that Guillén is concerned vitally with *union* "of man with the things on and above the planet, including woman and all other things." Joaquín Casalduero comments succinctly that *Cántico* is about "un hombre, la realidad, y el amor" ("a man, reality, and love"). Martha Miller writes: "Man's salvation depends upon his identification with the physical world; and this identification is made possible through love, which in turn takes on a magical power over the universe; paradoxically, love is supernatural for man because it joins him to nature."[23] This section is a consideration of the way in which Guillén perceives love to be an integral element of his vision of reality, and esteems love as a culmination of life, a type of symbolic eternity.

Guillén's poetic treatment of love, universally understandable and applicable, is always expressed in concrete and realistic terms. Love is an ideal to be sought and cherished, but is not idealized ("romanticized") to the point of becoming unreal or unattainable. Rather, love is a crucially important—quintessential—avenue to the goal of self-realization as conceived by the poet. And since the latter goal is natural and expected, so too is love. Consequently, love is a culmination within the overall context of fulfillment as the poet develops the idea throughout *Cántico*.

When writing of love, Guillén frequently favors the metonymic technique employed in poems on other subjects: he characteristically begins with a description of ordinary circumstances, which he then expounds overtly or metaphorically in a widely applicable generalization. The beloved is typically perceived as belonging to a larger ambience, of which she is also the culmination. Andrew P. Debicki comments on this type of situation: "La admiración que el protagonista siente ante el mundo encuentra expresión en su actitud ante la amada. En ella ve un ejemplo concreto de la perfección natural, y su amor por ella recoge y expresa su actitud entusiasmada ante la realidad" ("The admiration which the protagonist feels toward the world finds expression in his attitude toward the beloved. He sees in her a concrete example of natural perfection, and his love for her summarizes and expresses his enthusiastic attitude toward reality").[24]

Naturally enough, Guillén's frequently expressed predilection for concrete reality instead of intellectual abstractions is especially apparent in his love poetry. In "Preferida a Venus" [Preferred to Venus], he observes and applauds the vitality of a woman swimmer in her real, not mythical, humanity:

De las ondas,
Terminante perfil entre espumas sin forma,

Imprevista
Surge—lejos de su patria—la seducción marina.

¡Salve, tú
Que de la tierra vienes para ser en lo azul

No deidad
Soñada sino cuerpo de prodigio real!

Nadadora
Feliz va regalando desnudez a las ondas.

(*AN*, 299)

Among the waves
—far from her homeland—a seduction

appears unforeseen from the sea,
a precise outline in the formless foam.

Welcome to you,
come from the land to live in the blue sea,

not a fancied goddess
but a female form, a marvel, and real.

The swimmer,
joyous, gives her nudity to the waves.

In a sense, Guillén reverses his accustomed stylistic procedure in this poem, without changing his characteristic technique of applying a specific circumstance to a more universal idea. Here he recollects a mythical abstraction—the birth of Venus in the sea—and gives the idea incarnate reality by applying it to a woman swimmer. The title, "Preferred to Venus," expresses unequivocally the poet's sentiment as he contemplates the scene. In Guillén's view, of course, reality is always superior to cerebral abstractions. The real woman is therefore naturally preferable to the intellectual idea of the goddess. At the same time, it is important to note that the concrete situation—the woman in the waves—leads him to think of the eternal idea of the goddess contained in the myth. The real and ideal images are mutually enriching and complementary. The woman is preferable to the myth, but the mythical idea endows the present scene with a timeless truth.

Guillén's use of the word "nudity" in the last line of the poem is somewhat idiosyncratic. While the words "nudity" and "nude" are used literally, they frequently have a figurative meaning and indicate "purity," or freedom from any extraneous or irrelevant quality. So while he may be referring to a nude bather in the poem, he can also be assumed to have in mind her intense vitality as she moves among the waves. The poet also uses "nudity" and "nude" to refer to purity in nature or to natural phenomena; he does not use the words exclusively to describe human beings.[25]

Another characteristic of Guillén's love poetry is that it is frequently "erotic" or "sensuous" without necessarily being "sexual." The term "erotic" is used here in the broad sense of "pertaining to love," since Guillén writes much sensuous poetry that exhibits erotic feeling without any implication of sexual relations. "Preferred to Venus" is a representative expression of this type, but is by no means a unique example.

As mentioned, Guillén views love as an epitome of self-realization, often within the larger context of nature. Readers of Guillén's work are aware that the central theme of his well-known poem, "Salvación de la primavera" [A Springtime Salvation] is personal rebirth through love, paralleled by the springtime regeneration of nature. That eleven-page poem, a litany of love, is not reproduced here due to its length. In a much shorter poem, "Con nieve o sin nieve" [With or Without Snow], Guillén reveals his erotic view of *both* life and the beloved, and subject-object distinctions vanish in a vision of loving unity:

Ven a ver. La nieve
Cae más despacio.
El copo en desorden
Se demora, blando.

Quede en su blancura
La ciudad igual.
Para mí varía
Tu vivacidad.

Ya en este balcón
Sonríe esperando,
Ágil, pulcro, joven,
El frío más claro.

¡Diáfana alianza!
Frío con cristal.
Los dos, trasparentes,
Hacia la verdad.
. . . .

¿El mundo es inmenso?
Yo contigo aquí.
En tu abrazo gozo
Del sumo confín.
. . . .

La nieve exquisita
Se ofrece. Regalo
Nunca merecido:
Otro mundo intacto.

El cielo da cielos,

Incesante don.
¿Nieve? Yo la adoro.
Nos junta a los dos.

Nevadas cornisas,
Posibles palacios,
Tu amor en el centro,
Y el mundo nevado.

(*AN*, 48–49)

Come and see. The snow
is falling slowly.
The flakes linger
softly, in disorder.

The city can be uniform,
in its whiteness.
For me, *your* brightness
is variation enough.

Here on the balcony,
the clearest cold
smiles waiting,
lively, clean and fresh.

Such a clear union
of the cold and the window!
The clear pair of them, together,
toward the truth.
. . . .

The world is immense?
I am here with you.
In your embrace I enjoy
a supreme boundary.
. . . .

The exquisite snow
offers itself. It is
an unearned gift:
another, untouched world.

Ceaselessly, heaven gives
more heavens.
The snow? I adore it.

It joins us together.

Snowy cornices
—potential palaces—
your love in the center,
and the snow-covered world.

The attitude of the speaker in this poem is similar to that seen in poems dealing with the primacy of the natural world in Guillén's work. The poet is indoors, but senses a vital unity in the quality of "sameness" that is evident from the surrounding blanket of snow. Despite the winter season, there is a feeling of renewal which emerges from nature's mantle of pure whiteness (particularly in the third strophe), and the inner and outer worlds collaborate in creating a form of existential truth for the speaker.

The affirmation of the value of external reality and the poet's expressed feeling of oneness with it is, of course, typical of *Cántico*. The obvious difference between this poem and others used for previous discussion is the addition of a second person. She shares the poet's sense of participation in the world, and the two protagonists additionally participate in each other's joy. The chain of the relationship between the speaker, the world, and the beloved becomes somewhat circular. The poet is drawn to the world (first strophe), but equally to his companion (second strophe), with whom he shares his sense of oneness with the beyond (third and fourth strophes). He perceives another world—a microcosm—in the form of the woman (fifth strophe). The sensuous language of the sixth strophe is slightly ironic in a positive way: he speaks of the world as if *it* were a lover, then goes on to affirm (seventh strophe) that the world beyond the two of them gives them more to share between themselves.

The final strophe is a reaffirmation of the microcosmic-macrocosmic (or inner-outer) nature of the poet's vision, and underscores his thought that the woman is the culmination of all that he perceives ("your love in the center"). A notable aspect of the entire poem is the manner in which the speaker's attention shifts from inside to outside with little apparent distinction—the beloved is the central point of focus, but is not viewed as separate from the ambience. At the same time, the poet implies in the title, "With or Without Snow," that he does not depend on nature to appreciate the presence of the loved one.

"Relatedness" is a key term to understanding Guillén's expressed attitude. Just as he affirms and esteems the mutual participation of the individual and his surroundings, so woman enters his world as an equal and loving partner, and man and woman participate in one another as they do in all other things.

While Guillén does not romanticize love to the point of unreality, "With or Without Snow" is nevertheless an unquestionably romantic poem. The winter scene, the lovers, and the poet's positive attitude and descriptions all contribute to a portrait of ideal unity—this combination of the real and the ideal is always one of Guillén's most notable poetic traits. Being a "realist" in his outlook, however, Guillén does not require idyllic circumstances to inspire feelings of relatedness. He also perceives and appreciates love in the most ordinary of domestic situations. There is perhaps little "romantic" feeling associated with seeing one's lover occupied in the kitchen, but that is the theme of a succinctly expressed sentiment in "Amor de muchos días" [Love of Many Days]:

> Entre viandas, frutas, dulces, manteles, platos,
> Entre el hervir y el congelarse, tú misma, tú,
> Idéntica a tu forma feliz en los trabajos,
> Sin contraste, continua, sobre el esfuerzo tú.
>
> (*AN*, 308)

> Among the foods, fruits, sweets, tablecloths, dishes,
> between the boiling and freezing, you, you yourself,
> unchanging in your happy way with the chores,
> without contrast, persevering, above the stress, you.

Poems of this sort are perhaps more important for the implied attitude than for symbolic imagery. Indeed, there are no textual difficulties in this short poem, only an expression of caring. That the speaker retains and expresses his high esteem of the beloved even in the most prosaic of circumstances is an indirect comment on both of them, and on the solid foundation of their relationship. The speaker indicates appreciation of his companion in daily life, not only in "romantic" situations, and affirms the mutual support of lovers in times of crisis or hardship. His attitude toward the beloved, and hers toward him during an apparent political crisis, is declared calmly but vividly in "A pesar de todo" [In Spite of Everything]:

Sordos al atropello de voces y altavoces
En una batahola de pregón y cartel,
Extraños a la masa continua del bullicio,
—Montones que se ignoran entre el calor y el polvo—
A pesar de las redes invisibles del aire,
—Tanto crimen difuso, tanto cómplice ardid—
Se abrían paso a pie, despejaban su ruta,
Oyendo alrededor la algarabía amiga,
Gozando—sin mirar al cielo—del azul,
Seguros, implacables, los dos enamorados.

(*AN*, 326)

Deaf to the abuse of shouts and loudspeakers
in a din of proclamations and posters,
foreign to the endless mass of disturbance,
—ignorant crowds in the heat and dust—
in spite of the invisible traps in the air,
—widespread crime, accomplices and artifice—
[the lovers] made their way on foot, clearing their path,
hearing the friendly confusion around them,
enjoying the blue—without seeing the sky—
unfailing, implacable, the two lovers.

In *Cántico,* Guillén is vitally involved with the world around him, but in general he does not write about external *events;* such concerns become more visible in his later poetry. The protagonist or poetic conscience of *Cántico* is consummately humanitarian but more or less apolitical, and tends to concentrate on transcendent values and permanent truths. "In Spite of Everything" is therefore both a typical and an exceptional poem. It is concerned with people caught in a political upheaval, which in itself is unusual in *Cántico* (the poem first appears in the 1945 edition of *Cántico,* which would indicate that it was written either during the Spanish Civil War or World War II).

The more typical aspect of the poem is its affirmation of the lovers' mutual support, despite the circumstances in which they find themselves. Beginning with the title, Guillén chooses to emphasize their personal stability in the midst of social disintegration. While it is certainly unusual for Guillén to speak of love within the context of war, he employs the occasion to declare his valuation of love over less transcendent concerns.

The poem contains two noteworthy stylistic techniques. The ten lines of the poem form only one sentence, as if the speaker wished to express a stream of consciousness including both good and evil elements. At the same time, however, the specifically negative aspects appear parenthetically—between dashes—and the poem becomes much more positive in tone if it is reread and the lines in dashes omitted. The dominant elements are therefore those of love and support, characteristics that one expects to find in *Cántico*. The second stylistic element of note is that, unlike most of Guillén's intimate poetry, this poem is narrated in the third person. By not entering the poem himself, the speaker seems to imply that what matters in negative circumstances is the *ideal* of supportive love—both its reality and Platonic essence—that is attainable for those who treasure it, rather than a strictly personal experience.

The poems chosen for discussion so far in this section illustrate the most notable aspects of Guillén's attitude toward love in general: his insistence on the real woman as opposed to the unrealistic ideal, his vision of the beloved as a part of nature, and his affirmation of love in daily life and as a morally supportive force. The poems constitute a representative survey of the poet's ideas on love throughout *Cántico*, ideas which undergo some degree of evolution and change in his later work.

In addition to the foregoing ideas, there is a more intimate and personal side of Guillén's erotic poetry. Aside from poems expressing philosophical notions associated with his concept of love, Guillén has written some of the most expressive and touching love poetry of the twentieth century. His tender descriptions of intimacy and union between lovers express the intuited value and meaningfulness of love shared and appreciated equally by the partners. The idea of intuition is important in this regard, because Guillén's procedure is usually to convey a love-related feeling without belaboring the point he is making. In other words, the poet describes emotions that are profoundly significant, while at the same time avoiding obvious or overt sentimentality. Always aware of his *poetic* function, Guillén allows the reader to extract his own personal significance from the poetic idea. The short poem "Amor dormido" [Love Asleep] is characteristic of Guillén's tendency to suggest rather than expound when he writes of love and intimacy:

> Dormías, los brazos me tendiste y por sorpresa

Rodeaste mi insomnio. ¿Apartabas así
La noche desvelada, bajo la luna presa?
Tu soñar me envolvía, soñado me sentí.

(*AN*, 268)

You slept, reached out your arms to me, and by surprise you
encircled my sleeplessness. Were you thus pushing away
the sleepless night, beneath the captive moon?
Your dreaming surrounded me—I sensed that I was dreamed.

In four lines, the speaker implies several thoughts pertaining to relatedness and love. The peacefulness and trust of the beloved is the first element of note. Also in the first sentence, the speaker suggests the sense of togetherness that binds the couple, although one person is sleeping. By the naturalness of his description, the poet need not elaborate on the idea of a union between the lovers even when only one of them is conscious. The second sentence adds to the mood of the nocturnal scene. In the last line, the poet metaphorically reiterates the union between the two, varying the "flow" of the description from one person to the other. In the first sentence, the beloved reaches out to the speaker, while in the final line he enters her sphere of being through the metaphor of the dream. The mutuality of the union thus persists even while sleeping, as each partner nourishes the other.

Guillén's procedure is to suggest emotions and thoughts in which the reader participates, and this generalization applies to poems dealing with sexuality as the culmination of the lovers' expression for one another. That is not to say that Guillén considers sexuality to be the apogee of human love—life is not viewed so simplistically in *Cántico*, but is rather seen as *relation* in innumerable manifestations. Nevertheless, sexuality is love expressed in its most elemental form. Guillén sees a close relationship between spirit and corporeal nature, and so physical expression can contribute to self-realization for the lovers, together and as individuals.

Cántico contains several lengthy poems dealing with sexuality. The poem which follows, "Pleno amor" [Love Fulfilled], concentrates on the spiritual realization of love through an expression of the body. The lovers sacrifice egocentric intellect in an act of nature, and the momentary sacrifice of the ego leads to an increase in personal awareness and mutual love. The Roman numerals in the poem indicate Guillén's sections; other divisions of the text are for purposes of discussion:

I

¿Amor envuelve en las formas
De un viento? Se trasfigura
Bajo un viento nuestro abrazo:
Concentrándose está en lucha.
Triunfo habrá para los dos,
Gocémonos. ¡Oh, no hay burla
Contra la fe ya animal
De toda la criatura!
Desaparece la estancia.
Una luz de anhelo y súplica
Crea un ámbito al amor
Con muros de sombras juntas.
Infinita, sí, trascurre
La noche. Pero se ajusta
—Con la precisión de un mundo
Soñado por la absoluta
Claridad—a este clarísmo
Destino: nuestra ventura.
Y la ventura despacio
Va confiándose—nunca
Más estrellas en el cielo—
A una pesadumbre suya.
. . . .

(*AN*, 509)

I

Does love take form as the
wind and surround us? Our
embrace, concentrated in this struggle,
becomes transfigured in the wind.
Together we will triumph,
let us enjoy. There is no deception
against our instinctive,
creaturely faith.
The room vanishes.
A light of desire and yearning
creates an enclosure for love
with walls cast by joined shadows.
The infinite night
elapses. But it adjusts
—with the precision of a world

dreamed with absolute
clarity—to this brightest
destiny: our happiness.
And the happiness slowly
entrusts itself to its own burden
—and never was the sky
more filled with stars.

In these initial lines, the poet establishes two parallels which he maintains and develops throughout the poem. The most notable technique is Guillén's description of the relatedness between the lovers and external nature, seen previously in "With or Without Snow." Here the speaker gives the impression of adapting nature to his own vision—viewing the world as it reflects the lovers—rather than appreciating objective reality for its own sake. The poet sees the world as an intense and subjective reflection of his immediate experience. Thus the wind becomes somewhat "humanized" in the first two sentences, and the night "adjusts" itself to the attitude of the lovers. The reference to stars in the last line indicates a perceived connection between sexual gratification and the celestial realm of the firmament. The poet therefore establishes a bond between spirit and nature, and the instinctive act includes thoughts of the heavens.

The "triumph" of instinct is a central theme of the poem, though it is not developed extensively in the initial lines. The idea which the poet expresses is that it is a necessary part of life to give due attention to one's animal nature, which Guillén describes as "creaturely faith." To ignore such an integral component of one's humanity would result in an incomplete form of being in Guillén's view, and so he considers sexuality a vehicle for emotional fulfillment. The poet's conviction that bodily expression leads one to discover the soul is elaborated in the lines that follow:

Mientras—la carne es también
Alma, reina tu blancura—
Un ritmo acoge y acrece
La obstinación—¡qué profunda
Masa tanta noche en vela!—
De esta casi calentura,
De este buen ardor.
Palpitan,
Humildemente nocturnas,

Las estrellas como si
Regalasen una luna
De paz.
            Paz en la verdad.

(*AN*, 509–10)

At the same time—the flesh is also
spirit, and your whiteness prevails—
a rhythm welcomes and increases
the persistence of this near fever,
this full eagerness
—how deep
the night is, awake.
The stars,
meekly nocturnal,
sparkle as if
to present us a moon
of peace.
            Peace in the truth.

In these lines the poet begins to elaborate his earlier affirmation of "creaturely faith." Guillén introduces a central theme of the poem, the idea of arriving at one's spirit through an expression of the flesh. Having already established a parallel between the lovers and the stars—heavens—above them, the poet now declares his notion of spirituality in the lovers' act. He also reiterates the bond between the lovers and the night.

The culmination of this entire first section of the poem is a form of existential "truth" created by the lovers. Their love has its own intrinsic value, since it is an intimate and vital truth that is expressed as elementally as is humanly possible in the act of lovemaking. The idea of "truth" and its significance is developed more fully in the second half of the poem.

II

En la verdad.
                        Y se anuncia
Lo más fabuloso. ¿Tumba
Para una resurrección,
Para llegar a ser pluma
Casi indistinta del aire,
Aire sobre el mar, espuma
Que fuese nube en un cielo

Con voz de mar?
. . . .

(*AN*, 510)

II

In the truth.
And a fable
is announced. Is it a tomb
for a resurrection,
for becoming a feather
lost in the wind,
wind above the ocean, foam
which might be a cloud in a sky
with the sound of the sea?

In the second section of the poem, Guillén concentrates on the symbolic "annihilation" of egocentricity through surrender to the instinctual, "creaturely" act of love. The temporary sacrifice of the ego is rewarded by the overwhelming sense of communion with the beloved. Thus, the "tomb" mentioned is symbolic not of death but of rebirth, characterized by a sensation of liberation which the poet describes by using flight as a metaphor. The idea of "annihilation" of the ego is developed further in the following lines:

No hay más ruta
Que este más allá mortal:
Vértigo de una dulzura
Que de más vida en más vida
Se atropella, se derrumba,
. . . .

Y va a la noche desnuda
Con un ansia de catástrofe,
O de postrer paz, en fuga
Final ¿hacia qué reposos,
Qué aplanamientos, qué anchuras?
¿O hacia la aniquilación
Desesperada?
Concluya,
Concluya tanta inminencia.
Todo se confía—nunca
Más estrellas en el cielo—
A su pesadumbre muda,
Fatal.
. . . .

(*AN*, 510–11)

There is no other path
than this mortal beyond:
a vertigo of sweetness
which from more and more life
hurries headlong
and goes to the denuded night
with a longing for catastrophe
or concluding peace, in final
flight: toward what repose,
what leveling off, what widths?
Or toward desperate
annihilation?
Let the imminence conclude.
All entrusts itself to its
destined, mute burden
—and never was the sky
more filled with stars.

The poet concentrates here on the confused state of the ego during intercourse, a confusion reflected in the somewhat abrupt syntax of the long first sentence. The lovers approach the culmination of their sexual expression but the speaker does not attempt to characterize their ecstasy, choosing instead to voice his bewilderment during the "creaturely" act that ultimately nourishes the spirit. Even when describing the moment of climax, however, he reiterates his affirmation of the bond between the lovers and nature that appears throughout the poem.[26]

Guillén concludes the poem with a declaration of the spiritual fulfillment that results from the "abdication" of the ego during the instinctual expression of love:

¡Sea!
Fatalmente
Puede más que yo la angustia
Que me entrega a la catástrofe,
—Todo conmigo sucumba—
Que no será . . . que no es
Una catástrofe—¡brusca
Perfección!—por más que abdique,
Y se desplome y se hunda

—Amor, amor realizado—
El alma en su carne: puras.

(*AN*, 511)

Let it be!
The anxiety
which—stronger than I—fatefully
delivers me to the catastrophe
—let all else yield with me—
is not and will not be a catastrophe
but brusque perfection
—however the soul might
relinquish itself, collapse and plunge
in the flesh: purified
in consummated love.

These final lines summarize the dominant idea of the second half of the poem, the affirmatively ironic attitude that temporary sacrifice of the ego in the hierarchy of the mind results in an expansion of one's personal horizon by way of communion with the beloved. The act of nature adds to the fulfillment of the soul; as Guillén states in another erotic poem: "Sobrehumana, la arcilla" ("The clay is superhuman," *AN*, 182).

Guillén's approach to sexual love is in accord with his view of love and the world in general: a specific experience is lived, assimilated, and adds to his enrichment and life. Since *relation* is his primary concern and goal, it is not surprising that the poet should describe love with the same attitude that he demonstrates when describing a sunrise. Conversely, it is logical to affirm that the poet approaches all of life erotically, with feelings and emotions of love, since he considers life itself to be his lover.

Another aspect of Guillén's erotic poetry is that the lovers create a transcendent truth in his view. While the lovers are mortal, the truth that they create between them is a symbolic foil against death. One long poem concludes with the following rhetorical question: "¿Por vencida te das ahora, Muerte?" ("Do you now surrender, Death?" *AN*, 185).[27]

The poems reproduced for analysis here are indicative of the coherent yet multifacted unity of Guillén's love poetry. The idea of love combatting death is not a salient feature of the poet's erotic vision, but this notion is characteristic of Guillén's predilection for thoughts of life that give the individual a certain transcendence in the face of death. Death is accepted in Guillén's world, and the poet confronts death directly, without dwelling heavily on symbolic or religious solutions to mortality. That is the theme of the ensuing section.

IV *Time and Death*

Guillén concerns himself both intellectually and emotionally in *Cántico* with the concept of time and the reality of death, although the latter is not an overwhelming preoccupation. The attitudes which the poet expounds in *Cántico* undergo some modification in his second major work, *Clamor*, but the present discussion is centered on the ideas expressed in the poetry of *Cántico*. The intent in this section is to examine two notable areas of thought that Guillén tends to favor in his poems about time: the importance of the present moment in the life of the individual, and the cyclical and/or regenerative nature of the temporal march. The poet's attitude toward death is examined in the second part of the section.

The importance of the present resides in the belief that the individual must not continually inhabit a prospective "tomorrow" which slips into "yesterday" without having been truly experienced. Since *Cántico* is poetry and not philosophy, Guillén does not write on this subject in an interpretive or prescriptive manner. Instead, he indicates his feelings about the necessity of living fully in the present moment by describing his own affirmative experience.

"A lo largo de las orillas ilustres" [Along the Illustrious Shores] contrasts the feeling of history and historical significance with the *existential* importance of the present moment for the speaker. The poem has a particularly European tone, for the speaker feels the weight of a long historical tradition bearing down on him in a manner that seldom occurs to American readers. His sense of history appears in the title and throughout the poem, but his heart is in the present, here and now:

Río con riberas
De historias y mitos:
¿Dejas o te llevas
Los días perdidos?

Días . . . Y trascurren.
Un son va quedando

—Orillas ilustres—
Preso de un encanto.

Suenan con el río
Las voces de antes.
¡Fragancia de siglos
Frescos! Y la tarde.

Bajo los castaños
Se amontonan tomos
Para que despacio
Crezca el tiempo en ocio.

Entre monumentos
—Mayo en flor y puente—
Va el río queriendo
Siempre, siempre, siempre.

(*AN*, 96)

River with banks
of history and myth:
Do you leave behind or carry away
the bygone days?

The days pass.
Illustrious shores—
a sweet sound remains as
the captive of a spell.

Voices from the past
sound with the river.
The fragrance of
fresh centuries. And the afternoon.

Volumes collect
beneath the chestnut trees,
so that time grows
slowly and leisurely.

Amid the monuments of
a bridge and May in blossom,
the river goes wanting
forever, forever, forever.

The attitude of the poet is one of affirmative irony, since the river is itself a metaphor par excellence of passing time. As readers of Spanish literature are well aware, one of the most famous poems of the Spanish Middle Ages, Jorge Manrique's elegy on the death of his father, is based on the image of the flowing river. Guillén, of course, uses the same metaphor in his later poetry. In *Cántico*, however, the emphasis is on living, and on the timeless value of the present tense.

In his role as poet, Guillén maintains a degree of aesthetic distance from the image of the river, rendering his stress on the present more convincing. He achieves this aesthetic effect primarily by not identifying the scene of the narration. A native of Valladolid might write of the Duero—scene of some significant Spanish history—but that would cloud the poetic issue. Guillén chooses instead to mention *a* river and thus concentrate on the principal theme of the poem, his consciousness of the past compared and contrasted with the fullness of the present.

In the initial strophe, Guillén pays due homage to the historical importance of the river, then poses the rhetorical question that is answered and expounded in the rest of the poem. The speaker's own attitude begins to emerge in the second strophe, in which he refers to the "spell" of the present and relates it to the sound of the water—but now it is a sound that speaks to the poet at this moment, not an instant that flows away to the sea. The contrast is elaborated in the third strophe, as the poet creates a sonorous counterpoint of the voices from history and those of today, of this afternoon. He also looks toward the future in this strophe, referring briefly to "fresh centuries," to time in the making. The fourth strophe contains another allusion to historical time collected in history books.

The pleasant irony of the last strophe underscores the speaker's desire to place the present at the top of the historical hierarchy. The true monuments are not statues of monarchs and warriors, but the flowers of springtime and a bridge spanning the water. These two images indicate regeneration (spring) and movement through time (crossing the river). So while the poet is conscious of historical tradition, he is personally far more interested in what is happening on a springtime afternoon, for that is his own reality today.

The message of the poem, then, is that history can be given its due, but that the individual is alive in the present tense and must not lose sight of that crucially important fact. In another poem that treats the theme of the present, "Las doce en el reloj" [Twelve

O'clock, Noon], Guillén concentrates on the present as a culmination in time:

> Dije: Todo ya pleno.
> Un álamo vibró.
> Las hojas plateadas
> Sonaron con amor.
> Los verdes eran grises,
> El amor era sol.
> Entonces, mediodía,
> Un pájaro sumió
> Su cantar en el viento
> Con tal adoración
> Que se sintió cantada
> Bajo el viento la flor
> Crecida entre las mieses,
> Más altas. Era yo,
> Centro en aquel instante
> De tanto alrededor,
> Quien lo veía todo
> Completo para un dios.
> Dije: Todo, completo.
> ¡Las doce en el reloj!

(*AN*, 485)

> I said: all is now replete.
> A poplar stirred,
> rustling with love
> its silvery leaves
> of green and grey.
> Its love was the sun.
> Then, at noon,
> a bird immersed
> his song in the wind
> with such adoration
> that a flower
> in the tallest grain beneath the wind
> felt its praises sung.
> At that moment,
> I was the center
> of the surroundings,
> and saw that it was all
> complete for a god.
> I said: all is complete.
> Twelve o'clock, noon.

Here the poet's attitude is one of fulfillment in the present, a mood accentuated by the symmetry of the scene. (Geometrical imagery, a unique feature of Guillén's poetry, will be examined in the following section.) The hands of the clock point skyward to the sun at its zenith, and the speaker finds himself at the central point of the symmetrical ambience. His affirmation that he is at the center of the scene is similar to a declaration in "Beyond," where Guillén states that one's personal center is indeed "portable" in the sense that each individual is potentially capable of delineating his own center of conscious functioning and living within it.

The poet's own center forms part of the scene he describes. It is interesting to note that there is a continuum between the animal and plant kingdoms in the metaphorical joining of the bird and flower, which also symbolically unites the air and sky to the earth. The poet, as the central figure of the symmetrical whole, senses that there is a divinity to it, or at least a potential divinity ("complete for *a* god"). He does not enter into religious considerations, but is conscious of a transcendent value in the noontime scene.[28]

The poem deals with fulfillment or culmination, at a "complete" moment in time. But then, any moment is complete, for time and creation have reached their most advanced point of evolution at any given instant. This is seen in "Beyond," and in "Twelve O'clock, Noon" creation has reached a culmination at the time and place described in the poem. The value of the present is therefore not relative or teleological, but absolute, because at this moment creation has achieved the totality of its potential.

In the two poems discussed above, Guillén concentrates on expounding the necessity and joy of life in the present. The second salient attitude toward time found in *Cántico* involves futurity and potential. We live in the present, and history to be made lies before us. Guillén looks toward the future with hope and optimism, as potential self-realization for himself and others. Using the child as an image, he reveals his hope for the future in "Cuna, rosas, balcón" [Cradle, Roses, Balcony]:

> ¿Rosas? Pero el alba.
> . . . Y el recién nacido.
> (¡Qué guardada el alma!)
> Follajes ya: píos.

Muelle carne vaga,
Sueño en su espesura,
Cerrazón de calma,
Espera difusa.

Rosas—para el alba.
Pura sí, no alegre,
Se esboza la gracia.
¡Oh trémulas fuentes!

Creaciones, masa,
Desnudez, hoyuelos.
La facción exacta
Relega lo eterno.

¿Ya apuntan cerradas
Aún, sí, sonrisas?
. . . La aurora (¿Y el alba?)
¡Oh rosas henchidas!

(*AN*, 78)

Roses? But, the dawn.
And the newborn.
(How protected his soul is!)
And now there is foliage, and birds' song.

His soft flesh is idle
in a dense dream:
a stormy calm,
a diffuse waiting.

Roses for the dawn.
Not happy, but pure,
the beauty becomes outlined.
Ah, quivering fountains!

Creation, form,
nudity and dimples.
The eternal is obscured
by this face, here.

Smiles—still indirect—
do they become sharper?
. . . The aurora. (And the dawn?)
Ah, replete roses!

In this poem Guillén develops an elaborate metaphor establishing a parallel futurity in nature—represented by the dawn—and human futurity in the form of a newborn child. The two images are intentionally combined throughout the poem. The parallel themes are presented in the initial strophe, the child figure dominates the second, and nature (dawn and increasing clarity) is emphasized in the third.

The fourth strophe is a remarkable if indirect example of Guillén's predilection for the concrete and specific as opposed to the abstract. The initial reference to nature—creation, forms taking shape in the light—and the tiny figure of the unclothed child combines the macrocosm with humanity on a tiny scale, but the poet equates them in the same sentence. In the second sentence, Guillén extends the image by stating that the child's face—that is, immediate presence—is so imposing in its own reality that it "obscures" or "relegates" the outside macrocosm to a secondary position. That is not to say, of course, that the outside world is unimportant, but here the miracle of human life and potentiality receives the poet's priority.

The final strophe contains another reference to futurity, with the added element of awakening consciousness. The child's diffuse attention begins to focus, at least potentially. Here again, Guillén places the child at the top of his hierarchy in this particular poem: the infant's coming to conscious clarity is characterized as an "aurora," while the dawn is mentioned parenthetically. Here Guillén's stylistics and choice of words infuse the child image with added meaning. The infant's consciousness is placed before the dawn, and the poet characterizes the sharpening attention as an "aurora." Since this word derives from Aurora, the Roman goddess of the dawn, the child's budding smile is elevated to a status approaching divinity. Guillén completes the extended metaphor by again referring to the dawn and repeating the image of the rose, a traditional symbol of both futurity and perfection.

The poem is especially notable for the combination of natural and human elements that Guillén joins in order to convey the message of futurity and potential. Nature and humanity are never far apart in *Cántico,* and in this poem they complement one another in direct but sophisticated imagery. In another poem on the theme of time, "Los jardines" [The Gardens], Guillén uses natural elements to develop the idea that the present always carries the bud of the future within itself. In this case, he looks at childhood or its memory, and at the time continuum which the child and the adult can represent:

> Tiempo en profundidad: está en jardines.
> Mira cómo se posa. Ya se ahonda.
> Ya es tuyo su interior. ¡Qué trasparencia
> De muchas tardes, para siempre juntas!
> Sí, tu niñez, ya fábula de fuentes.
>
> (*AN*, 325)

> The profundity of time is there—in gardens.
> See how it slows, and then it deepens.
> Its inner essence is yours. What clarity
> of many afternoons, joined forever!
> Your childhood, yes, a fable of fountains.

The discussion of time to this point has been concentrated on Guillén's vision of the present as having absolute value, and the idea of futurity represented especially by the child figure. In "The Gardens," the two ideas are joined to a certain extent, with the notable difference that the perspective is that of an adult looking back at childhood and realizing that it has flowed into the present moment. The poem deals with beginnings, but from the point of view of a speaker who is looking at his own origins. The idea of source or origin is inherent in the two main images of the poem, a garden with a fountain that is perhaps the central focal point. The scene has archetypal connotations, as both the garden and fountain are age-old symbols of primordial beginnings.[29] Guillén therefore takes a specific scene and endows it with universal meaning for the reader.

Once the symbolic functions of the garden and its fountain are understood, the poetic description of time itself becomes clearer. In the garden, one can metaphorically "see" into the "depths" of time—that is, back to one's own origins. In the second line, the speaker appears to transcend the arbitrary units of clock time and penetrate the temporal continuum so as to perceive its essential oneness. That oneness or indivisibility is salient in lines 3–4. The idea of these sentences is that the "inner essence" of time is indeed its unity. Indivisibility, then, is the "being" of time. So the speaker's origin or childhood, emanating from the fountain at the center of the garden, is with him still, for the days of his life are in essence one, not many.

The word "fable" is itself of interest, given Guillén's erudition in matters of language and style. Although this word has come to mean primarily a fantasy or moral story, etymologically it can refer to any dramatic composition or narrative. One's life drama—fable—therefore begins at the fountain, and in this case the drama of life has a mythic quality to it, as one looks back to the symbolic source that is still intrinsically vital in the present.[30]

The idea of a temporal continuum as opposed to a linear march is also applicable to the adult who looks *ahead* in time as well as back to his origins. "Advenimiento" [Advent] is a poem in which the speaker appears as the sum total of his previous experience, and looks toward future personal renewal as the world is reborn in springtime:

¡Oh luna, cuánto abril,
Qué vasto y dulce el aire!
Todo lo que perdí
Volverá con las aves.

Sí, con las avecillas
Que en coro de alborada
Pían y pían, pían
Sin designio de gracia.

La luna está muy cerca,
Quieta en el aire nuestro.
El que yo fui me espera
Bajo mis pensamientos.

Cantará el ruiseñor
En la cima del ansia.
Arrebol, arrebol
Entre el cielo y las auras.

¿Y se perdió aquel tiempo
Que yo perdí? La mano
Dispone, dios ligero,
De esta luna sin año.

(*AN*, 57)

The moon, *such* presence of April—
how vast and sweet is the air!
All that I lost

will return, along with the birds.

Yes—with the birds
that in a morning chorus
sing and sing and sing
in disorder.

The moon is very close and
still in this, our air.
My past, behind my present thoughts,
awaits me.

At the peak of desire
a nightingale will sing.
[There are] rich red clouds,
between the breeze and the heavens.

And is that past of mine
lost in oblivion? My hand,
such a nimble god, directs
this ageless moon.

The themes of childhood and springtime are familiar from other poems in which Guillén treats the problem or concept of time. The present poem differs from others studied in this section in that here the main theme is not the present moment or the future, but a combination of these ideas presented in the form of personal renewal. It is also important to remember that, in the work of a sophisticated poet, an image or metaphor rarely has the same connotation in all contexts. Thus in the first poem considered in this section, "Along the Illustrious Shores," a day in May is seen primarily as vital reality in the present, as compared with the monumental but bygone historical events of the past. Similarly, the view of one's own past that appears in "The Gardens" expounds the theme of temporal unity. In "Advent," on the other hand, spring means regeneration in nature that is paralleled in the individual, and the past is seen as one's personal "baggage" that accompanies him on his voyage into the future.

The title, "Advent," has religious overtones, notable in that much religious ritual is involved with rebirth and renewal. In this poem, renewal takes place on a personal level and is reflected in the ambience surrounding the speaker. Nature regenerates itself in springtime—April and the returning migratory birds—and the dawn of a new day represents primordial beginnings as well (cf. "Beyond"). The image of the birds also has a quasi-religious connotation in that birds are a traditional symbol of transcendent spirit. Guillén relates them to the natural surroundings, however, by mentioning indirectly in the second strophe that they are obeying laws of instinct, not spirit, in their migration and song—and so they sing "in disorder."

Regeneration in nature is portrayed via the images of springtime, the birds, and the dawn of a new day. The parallel situation is of course that of the poet, who speaks of his own renewal in the first, third, and fifth strophes. For rhetorical purposes, he uses the natural analogy of winter as a dormant season, alluding to what he "lost" as returning to him in the spring.[31] He then directs his attention forward, as his past experience forms part of his renewal.

The third strophe contains an additional parallel between the poet and nature. The moon, another object of cyclical rebirth, is not seen in terms of the vastness of outer space, but symbolically forms a part of the earthly ecosystem. The heavens are brought to earth, just as nature in this poem reflects a human disposition.[32]

In the final strophe, the poet reiterates that his primary interest is permanence rather than change. He begins with a rhetorical question that is then all but ignored in the concluding sentence which makes an apparent reference to the speaker's consciousness of his function as poet. As seen in "Beyond" and in other poems yet to be discussed (in section 6), Guillén views poetry as a means of saving the past and present from oblivion. The past is not lost, nor is the moon this April, because the poet is there to record it in writing. The hand is therefore in control of the situation and confers permanence on the scene. Nature regenerates itself, and the speaker as man participates in the renewal, while as poet he preserves the moment for us, his readers.

In summarizing Guillén's attitude toward the concept of time as a topic of consideration in poetry, it is perhaps most relevant to note that, in *Cántico,* he departs significantly from traditional Occidental thought about the march of time and about humanity as being fundamentally and essentially historical. In his poems treating the problem of time, Guillén is most concerned with the vitality of the present, with the temporal flow as a continuing process, and with futurity and renewal. His stated preference for themes of permanence does not mean, however, that he is oblivious to clock time or the march of time toward death.

The reality and inevitability of human finitude is confronted directly in *Cántico*, but it is not a dwelling point. There is no grim fascination with the mystery of death, as one finds in the work of Guillén's friend Lorca, nor is death as an existential problem developed philosophically or systematically, as in the work of Unamuno. Rather, Guillén seems to note his own mortality on a clear but distant horizon, study it briefly, and dismiss it in favor of other themes. The attitude found in *Cántico* changes in later works, especially *We Will End at the Sea*, though not as radically as one might initially suspect.

Limitations of space preclude a consideration of all aspects of death as the subject appears in *Cántico*. There are poems in which death is considered as a phenomenon, almost a curiosity, by a somewhat dispassionate observer, as well as a poem in which the speaker expresses the traditional idea that individuals live on through their children.[33] In the three poems chosen for discussion here, the poet's theme is his own personal mortality. The poems constitute Guillén's most intimate expression on the subject of death in *Cántico*, for they reflect the meditations of a profoundly sensitive poet as he gazes into his own mortal mirror. Prior to discussing these poems, it will be profitable to examine briefly Guillén's attitude toward a Supreme Being and afterlife, and also a contemporary existential philosophy with which the poet is in at least partial accord.

Agnosticism is the attitude that prevails in *Cántico* and in Guillén's later work as well. But this is an attitude, not a systematically developed outlook. Unlike Unamuno, for example, Guillén does not belabor or flaunt his agnosticism. For reasons of his own which are not expressed in detail in his work, Guillén does not accept a doctrinal view of God and human life. On the other hand, he is undoubtedly predisposed toward belief in God, as he stated in a published interview: "Se puede estar con Dios o sin Dios, pero nunca contra el posible Dios" ("One can be with or without God, but never against the possible God").[34] The *possible* presence of God is seen in a poem discussed above, "Twelve O'clock, Noon," in which the poet intuits a divine transcendence in the scene described. Guillén also states in conversation that he does not adhere to any sectarian religious view of divinity or afterlife, though he refers to himself as a "cultural Catholic," an attitude easy to appreciate in a Spaniard from Old Castile.[35]

Insofar as Guillén's attitudes toward death can be categorized and/or intellectualized in philosophical terms, the most approximate frame of reference is probably afforded by the German existentialist philosopher Martin Heidegger. There is naturally no methodical presentation of Heidegger's thought in Guillén's poetry; Professor Guillén once stated in conversation that he was not familiar with Heidegger's philosophy in any detail. Nonetheless, there are three key points in Heidegger's main work, *Being and Time*, with which Guillén is in essential agreement, and which may help to clarify Guillén's views by providing an additional perspective. The three concepts relevant to the outlook expressed in *Cántico* can be summarized as follows: (1) of all the innumerable possibilities which one confronts in a lifetime, death is the supreme or ultimate possibility, for it is the most personal and the most unavoidable; (2) it is essential to confront and accept without illusion the inevitability and unavoidability of death if one is to live authentically, that is, live without attempting futilely to avoid the issue; and (3) by accepting one's own finitude, it is possible to attain a measure of freedom from death by rising above the pettiness of inauthenticity.[36]

Heidegger might be further summarized in the following philosophical equation: existential awareness of death plus acceptance of death equals freedom from death through authentic life. Acceptance is an essential prerequisite of authenticity, for if one does not fully accept the reality of death, authenticity is sacrificed to illusions as one seeks to avoid confronting this most personal of all possible issues.

Guillén does not concern himself with developing a philosophy of mortality, for he is far more interested in life here and now, as seen in several poems discussed above. But mortality is confronted and accepted realistically and willingly as part of life, which gives the poet some common ground with the philosopher. In "La cabeza" [The Head], the speaker puts his hand to his forehead, and comments on the realization of the mortal body that rests beneath the veneer of vitality that he feels:

> ¡Tierno canto de la frente,
> Batido por tanta onda!
> La palma presume monda
> La calavera inminente.
> Si la tez dice que miente
> El tacto en ese barrunto,

Porque a un gran primor en punto
—Ápice de su matiz—
Conduce la piel feliz,
Palpa el hueso ya difunto.

(*AN*, 243)

The tender edge of the forehead,
altered by many waves [of flesh].
The palm detects the pure
imminence of the skull.
If the bright complexion belies
the foreboding touch [of the hand]
because the lively flesh
indicates exact exquisiteness
and the delicacy of the facial hues
—[the hand] feels the bone of the deceased.

During the simple act of placing his hand to his forehead, the poet becomes acutely aware of the fact that, beneath the thin layer of living flesh, lies the skull, the perennial image of human mortality. In this context, it is useful to distinguish between an abstract or intellectual awareness of death, and the intense *personal* recognition of one's own finitude. The latter attitude appears to be the case in the present poem, in which the speaker declares that he is aware of his own mortal remains in the form of the skull. Stylistically, Guillén emphasizes his point by using the forehead, a point at which the skeletal structure of the body is particularly apparent to the touch. This image, combined with the traditional significance of the skull, leads the reader to a sympathetic reading and understanding of the poet's mortal awareness.

The poem reflects at least one other idea that is in keeping with Guillén's characteristic attitudes. There is no mention of afterlife, but an impressive awareness of his personal certain death, a recognition in substantial agreement with Heidegger's notion that one must accept the reality of his own ultimate fate. Heidegger states that abstract realizations or platitudes such as "one dies" are not indicative of personal confrontation with finitude.[37] In "The Head," however, Guillén shows that his own vision of life includes an intense personal awareness of mortality.

Guillén's best-known poem about death is a sonnet entitled "Muerte a lo lejos" [Death in the Distance]. Here Guillén employs the classic sonnet form, presenting the problem in the first two quatrains of the sonnet, then giving the solution as he sees it in the concluding tercets. It is fitting that Guillén's most famous commentary on death should appear in the poetic form traditionally reserved for eternal themes and concerns. The poem is prefaced by an epigraph from Valéry, "Je soutenais l'éclat de la mort toute pure" ("I withstood the brilliant flash of purest death"):

Alguna vez me angustia una certeza,
Y ante mí se estremece mi futuro.
Acechándolo está de pronto un muro
Del arrabal final en que tropieza ·

La luz del campo. ¿Mas habrá tristeza
Si la desnuda el sol? No, no hay apuro
Todavía. Lo urgente es el maduro
Fruto. La mano ya lo descorteza.

. . . Y un día entre los días el más triste
Será. Tenderse deberá la mano
Sin afán. Y acatando el inminente

Poder diré sin lágrimas: embiste,
Justa fatalidad. El muro cano
Va a imponerme su ley, no su accidente.

(*AN*, 291)

At times I am anguished by a certainty
and my future trembles before me,
for it is suddenly surrounded by a wall
of that last [human] district where the

sunlight falls incidentally. [The certainty,] will it cause more sorrow
if bared by the sun? No, there is not yet anguish,
not yet. Far more urgent is the ripened
fruit that my hand reaches.

. . . And, of all my days, one will be the saddest.
My hand will unfold, without purpose.
And revering the imminent

force I shall say without tears: advance,
just destiny. The bleached wall
will impose on me its law, not its capricious chance.

As in "The Head," the speaker in "Death in the Distance" acknowledges his own mortality. Unlike the seemingly sudden realization of the previous poem, however, the attitude here is more intellectual or meditative in nature. The poet contemplates at some length his personal finitude, deciding and explaining quite lucidly and precisely what his attitude will be.

"Death in the Distance" shares with "The Head" an absence of religious considerations surrounding death. The temporal or biological limits of the poet's life are demarcated by a wall, and he does not attempt to see over the edge and glimpse the possibility of life continuing beyond his human boundaries. This attitude is another point that Guillén has in common with Heidegger, who posits that death must be accepted as an unmitigated annihilation and not with any conscious or unconscious desire to circumvent the issue.[38]

The images of the poem are both traditional and direct. The physical wall surrounding the speaker is easily equated with the limits of his life. The sunlight is "incidental" in the zone of death (lines 4–5) since it is, for once, useless. The idea of "useless" sunlight gives emphasis to the impression of finality, especially if the reader bears in mind the importance of light and clarity in Guillén's poetry. But the sunlight—light as comprehension—reveals clearly to the poet his impending fate. He acknowledges the situation and then turns his attention elsewhere, using another traditional metaphor, the ripened fruit of a tree, to indicate the rewards of his own maturity.

The final six lines of the poem expand the ideas expressed in the initial two strophes, particularly regarding the acceptance of death. The hand, which in the second strophe is the agent of the poet's desire or will, is seen to be still and lifeless in the future. But the poet willingly acknowledges natural law: in the final line, he sees death with resignation and clear assent. He has participated in life with full joy and enthusiasm, and his vital jubilation enables him to recognize death as a natural and just conclusion. Regarding acceptance, there is an interesting stylistic change in the 1945 edition of *Cántico*. In the early versions of the poem, the last strophe contains the phrase "diré con lágrimas" ("I shall say with tears"), which Guillén changes slightly but significantly to "*sin* lágrimas" ("*without* tears"), thus emphasizing the attitude of resigned acceptance on the part of the speaker.[39]

A relevant point made by Heidegger and mentioned above is that acceptance of the reality of death can result in a form of liberation, for such acceptance frees the individual from "inauthentic" life (avoidance) and allows one to live in a more fulfilled manner. Guillén shows himself to be in agreement with this notion in a characteristically optimistic poem entitled "Una sola vez" [Only Once]:

Muerte: para ti no vivo.

¿Mientras, aguardando ya,
Habré de ahogarme en congojas
Diminutas soplo a soplo?

Espera.
¡Sólo una vez,
De una vez!
Espera tú.

¿Ves cómo el hombre persigue,
Por el aire del verano,
Más verano de otro ardor?

Vivo: busco ese tesoro.

(*AN*, 334)

Death: I live not for you.

Shall I wait, and in the meantime
repress myself with petty
anguish, breath by breath?

You wait.
Only once,
in one blow!
You, wait.

Do you see how man pursues,
through the summer air,
a more intense, more burning season?

I live: I seek that treasure.

This poem, thematically similar to "Death in the Distance," presents a notable shift in the poet's focus. In the previous poem, the tone is primarily meditative, and the dominant attitude is that inevitability still allows for enjoyment of the ripened fruit of maturity. In "Only Once," the poet appears less contemplative or philosophical, addressing death directly and seeming to dismiss it almost defiantly in favor of the pursuits of his life at the moment, on this summer day. While the theme of the previous poem is unquestionably death, here the theme is equally clearly life, and death is not allowed to interfere.

The idea of existential "authenticity" is also relevant to "Only Once." By accepting the reality of death, the speaker is able to free himself from anguish, and not spend his life in "fear and trembling." He can instead devote himself to the pursuit of his own ideals, as he states in the two concluding sentences. These lines exhibit a Platonic attitude. The poet finds himself in a given situation—a summer day—and thinks of the spiritual essence of the day, the Platonic ideal or spiritual reality that lies beyond the physical ambience. Without depreciating the reality that surrounds him, the poet seeks to add to it with his own sense of idealism. So the conclusion of the poem is actually quite removed from thoughts of death, although death is initially the subject matter. Due to his acceptance of his human condition, the poet is not fearful, but is able to transcend himself in other, more fulfilling, directions.

Fulfillment, death notwithstanding, is the fundamentally dominant theme in *Cántico*. Death is, after all, not an overriding preoccupation for Guillén. The subject is never avoided, but does not account for much space in a five-hundred-page book. In a philosophy such as Heidegger's, death determines the entire world view, while Guillén takes appropriate notice and then directs his attention elsewhere. The following section studies Guillén's unique poetic expression of his vision of fulfillment in life.

V *The Symbolism of Wholeness*

Personal fulfillment is the common thread which joins the varied themes of *Cántico*. The poet's joyous "yes" to life is apparent regardless of the topic treated in any specific poem. Fulfillment is usually seen in varying degrees of directness or clarity as different life situations are presented by the poet. It will be enlightening to examine the singular manner in which Guillén expresses directly in *Cántico* his understanding of the ideal of personal transcendence and self-realization.

To convey via poetic imagery his sense of fulfillment in life, Guillén often employs geometrical figures and images that are generally, but not exclusively, circular in form. The circle is a natural symbol of wholeness since it comprises an enclosed totality which has no beginning or end, and therefore represents permanence as well as self-realized integration of the personality. The aesthetic elaboration of geometrical figures of totality probably reaches its most highly developed form in the Oriental mandala image, and the relationship between these archetypal figures and Guillén's poetry will be studied below. Guillén's critics have frequently noted the parallel that exists between circular imagery and the idea of unity in *Cántico*.[40] The following analysis seeks to illuminate and demonstrate the universality of Guillén's geometrical imagery of wholeness. Initially, it will be profitable to examine briefly the idea of *limits* that the poet espouses in *Cántico*.

A basic premise of *Cántico* is the necessity for identification with a particular mode of life, an idea which does not imply personal limitations in a negative sense. It is, rather, a realization that one cannot be all things, and there is no "upper" limit to the heights that can be attained once the individual becomes self-delineated. In "Beyond," Guillén declares that the objects of his ambience "limit and center" him (*AN*, 26), an affirmation of the primacy of external reality in *Cántico*. In the present context, the important message of this phrase is that the surrounding objects of the environment help the individual to define himself in the world. Another implication, stated directly in numerous poems, is satisfaction with one's circumstances. The attitude contrasts with much romantic expression, for example, in which present time and place are rarely seen as adequate for the realization of one's ideals.

Two poems will serve to illustrate the idea of limits that Guillén affirms. In the first of these, "Tornasol" [Iridescence], the poet applies his feeling for the necessity of limits to the formlessness perceived in the sky as he conceives the poem. He compares the sky to a limitless ocean, which would achieve more definition with the boundaries of a lake:

> Tras de las persianas
> Verdes, el verdor
> De aquella enramada
> Toda tornasol

Multiplica en pintas,
Rubias del vaivén
De lumbre del día,
Una vaga red

Varia que, al trasluz
Trémulo del estío,
Hacia el sol azul
Ondea los visos

Informes de un mar
Con ansia de lago
Quieto, claridad
En un solo plano,

Donde esté presente
—Como un firme sí
Que responda siempre
Total—el confín.

(*AN*, 86)

Through the green blinds
—all iridescence—
the greenness of that arbor
multiplies spottily
—a golden motion
of the light of day—
a wavering net

which, against the diffused
summer sunshine,
sends toward the blue sun

the formless radiance
of a sea
longing to be a quiet lake
—clarity on a single plane—

where there might be present
—like a firm yes
answering always in totality—
a limiting horizon.

The poem is a model example of Guillén's superb control of language. Its twenty lines constitute one sentence; a simplified translation of the complex syntax reads as follows: "Through the green blinds, the greenness multiplies a wavering net which sends toward the sun the formless radiance of a sea longing to be a lake, where a limiting horizon might be present." The extended metaphor of the poem reflects Guillén's belief in the necessity of limits in life. The speaker, standing under a tree, looks up at the diffuse sunlight as it filters through the foliage—the light and foliage together form the "wavering net" referred to in line 5. The flickering light—"formless radiance"—becomes a metaphor of formlessness in general, which here acquires a mildly negative significance. The sky is poetically seen as a sea without limits or form, meaning that it lacks definition. For this reason, the "sea" of the sky desires—"longs"—to be a lake with a limiting boundary. The final strophe therefore affirms the idea of limits: a "limiting horizon" would constitute a "firm yes," a "totality."

The metaphor of the sky refers, then, to the affirmation of limits in life as a necessary element of definition and form. In "Iridescence," the idea is applied to the natural world and the poet is an observer. In the poem below, "Casa con dos patios" [House with Two Patios], Guillén adopts a more personal tone, as he considers the enclosure of a patio:

Siempre seré el forastero
Que ve junto a la cancela
Cómo en el patio primero
Mármol frío
Vela
Por el señorío.
Pero aquel patio segundo
Con su cielo—tierra
Con sol—me envuelve en un mundo
Que pasma, ciñe y se cierra.

(*AN*, 262)

I will always be the outsider
who, beside the gate, sees
how in the first patio
cold marble
watches
over the mansion.
But the second patio
with its heaven above—earth

and sunlight—surrounds me in a world
that astounds, envelops and encloses.

The speaker presumably alludes to the fact that many large Spanish homes have two patios: a formal patio of exact, sculptured appearance, and an informal patio that is gardenlike and therefore closer to a natural state. The poet devotes a sentence to each patio. He feels no attraction toward the formal patio—he refers to it as "cold marble," and to himself as an "outsider" who has no intention of entering it. The formality of the first patio is further emphasized by stating that it belongs to the "señorío," itself a formal word that indicates a mansion or stately residence.

The second patio, which resembles a garden, is much more attractive: nature is relatively undisturbed, and the poet relates to natural life easily in this patio because of the qualities enumerated. Limits are not mentioned specifically, but the words chosen to describe the patio—surrounds, envelops, encloses—refer unequivocally to delineation and definition. The garden becomes a microcosm—a world in miniature—within which the speaker can move comfortably and establish his own personal center.

Guillén does not mention *symmetry* in the poem, but an image of symmetry is inherent in the idea of an enclosed garden. A symmetrical enclosure is the basic form of the mandala, an archetypal symbol of wholeness in the personality. Geometrical imagery is a universal expression representing wholeness, and can be profitably applied to Guillén's poetry.[41] Prior to such an examination, however, it will be valuable to examine briefly the mandala principle itself.

The word "mandala" derives from Sanskrit "circle." As objects of faith, Oriental mandalas are analogous to Christian crosses, in that they are used to stimulate and assist meditation.[42] Mandalas are occasionally painted on walls, but more often they are drawn on the ground. The believer "enters" the mandala for meditation, becoming enclosed within a symbolic microcosm; this idea is not unlike Guillén's description of the "world" created by the garden walls. Mandala symbolism is also extensive in the Occident, though it goes by no particular name. Traditional Christian art frequently exhibits mandala patterns, with emphasis placed on figures of symmetrical quaternity as well as on circular patterns. The rose windows of European cathedrals are perhaps the most spectacular examples of this type of artistic imagery.

As is the case with most aesthetic expression, mandala symbolism in our century has tended toward secularization. The mandala as a statement of totality or wholeness in the personality was studied theoretically by C. G. Jung, who elucidates its use by individuals who see no necessary parallel between the mandala and formal religious practice.[43] This nondogmatic use of geometrical imagery, typical of Guillén's work, produces three types of mandala symbolism that the poet favors: patterns of totality in nature, in the individual, and in humanity as a whole.

Mandala patterns in nature are seen in the symmetrical ordering of the earth and heavens. "Perfección" [Perfection] is one of Guillén's earliest and best-known poems; its early date (begun in 1926) indicates that symmetrical patterns form an integral part of *Cántico* throughout its development. In "Perfection," the individual sense of ordered totality is applied to the macrocosm of nature:

Queda curvo el firmamento,
Compacto azul, sobre el día.
Es el redondeamiento
Del esplendor: mediodía.
Todo es cúpula. Reposa,
Central sin querer, la rosa,
A un sol en cenit sujeta.
Y tanto se da el presente
Que el pie caminante siente
La integridad del planeta.

(*AN*, 250)

The firmament is curved,
compact and blue, above the day.
The splendor
becomes circular: midday.
All is a cupola. A rose
lies at the center indifferently,
subject to the sun at its zenith.
And the present moment is such
that the passerby senses
the totality of the planet.

This poem is similar in mood to "Twelve O'clock, Noon," sharing the vision of the noon hour as an almost magical moment when life becomes fulfilled and complete. In the former poem, the speaker senses himself to be at the center of the surrounding symmetry, whereas in "Perfection," the emphasis is on nature. The rose, itself a traditional symbol of perfection, is the centerpiece of the scene. The noon hour intensifies the image of symmetry as the sun is at its zenith in the dome of the firmament. Guillén utilizes a common optical illusion, the rounded appearance of the sky, to add to the feeling of circular totality dominated by the sun. The symbolic intensity of the situation is such that the present moment becomes pregnant with meaning for the poet. Although the poem deals with nature, the speaker or traveler through time is able to sense and participate in the unity of the cosmos at this moment. The Spanish word "integridad" (last line) derives from "entero," meaning "whole," and it is indeed the unity or wholeness of life that becomes manifest this noon hour.

If nature's symbol of flawlessness, the rose, is the central element of "Perfection," the individual person can also find himself surrounded by symmetrical wholeness, as in "Twelve O'clock, Noon," and in another aptly entitled poem, "Equilibrio" [Balance]:

> Es una maravilla respirar lo más claro.
> Veo a través del aire la inocencia absoluta,
> Y si la luz se posa como una paz sin peso,
> El alma es quien gravita con creciente volumen.
> Todo se rinde al ánimo de un sosiego imperioso.
> A mis ojos tranquilos más blancura da el muro,
> Entre esas rejas verdes lo diario es lo bello,
> Sobre la mies la brisa como una forma ondula,
> Hasta el silencio impone su limpidez concreta.
> Todo me obliga a ser centro del equilibrio.
>
> (*AN*, 318)

> It is a marvel to breathe in the clarity.
> In the air I see pure innocence,
> and as the sunlight wanes in a weightless peace,
> the soul grows with increasing volume.
> All is subdued by the spirit of stately calm.
> The wall gives more whiteness to my peaceful vision,
> the normalcy is beautiful, through those green gates;
> the breeze moves like a living form over the grain,
> even the silence imposes its concrete clarity.
> The whole obliges me to be the center of the balance.

The poem employs suggestion and tone in the manner of an impressionistic painting, providing the evocation of a mood, rather than the description of a sensation or event. The two natural elements dominating the poem are light and air, and the tone is most notably one of tranquility and, of course, balance. The "limits" in the poem are established by the wall surrounding the speaker. The poet surveys the tranquil scene and notes that he is at its center, as he states in the last line.

The symbolic aspect of the poem appears initially in line 4, as the poet's perception begins to shift from external to internal reality, represented by the "growth" of the soul. The emphasis on internal vision is sustained in line 6, in which the wall is seen to have more intense whiteness than in its natural state. That is to say that, as a symbolic object, the wall represents more than it *is* as an object in the world. Here the wall signifies the intuition of limits for the poet, allowing him to move comfortably within the delineated area that is certainly more psychological than physical. The various elements of the poem—natural and human—are joined in the last line. The speaker himself is now the focal point, as he senses that he is at the center of the surrounding symmetry. "Balance" or "equilibrium" is a way of expressing symmetrical wholeness, and here the balance is created by the speaker's own presence at the center of the scene.

In another poem, "Plaza mayor" [Main Square], the perception of mandala symbolism is applied to mankind as a whole. The title suggests collectivity, and the poem deals metaphorically with historical progress:

Calles me conducen, calles.
¿Adónde me llevarán?

A otras esquinas suceden
Otras como si el azar
Fuese un alarife sabio
Que edificara al compás
De un caos infuso dentro
De esta plena realidad.

Calles, atrios, costanillas
Por donde los siglos van
Entre hierros y cristales,
Entre más piedra y más cal.

Decid, muros de altivez,
Tapias de serenidad,

Grises de viento y granito,
Ocres de sol y de pan:
¿Adónde aún, hacia dónde
Con los siglos tanto andar?

De pronto, cuatro son uno.
Victoria: bella unidad.

(*AN*, 473)

Streets, streets guide me.
Where will they lead?

Corners follow
corners as if fate
were a wise designer
who had built here in harmony,
with an inspired chaos, within
this replete reality.

Streets, great halls, hillsides,
where the centuries wind
through iron and windows,
through more mortar and more stone.

Speak, proud walls,
quiet earthen walls,
grays of wind and granite,
ochers of bread and the sun:
Where now, toward what
do the centuries of walking lead?

Suddenly, four become one.
Victory: exquisite unity.

While geometrical imagery relates this poem to those discussed previously, the subject matter of "Main Square" varies in that here, the speaker considers himself to be representative of his culture, and sees himself as a member of society. Throughout the poem, a parallel is drawn between the speaker's route in the present and historical progress in the past. The poem concerns the common goals and aspirations of humanity, symbolized by the city with the main square at its center. Guillén begins with a rhetorical question that is answered in the rest of the poem. The second strophe deals with space—the march of humanity during the construction of its chaotic yet harmonious collective projects and ideals. This collectivity is the poet's reality at the moment, characteristically qualified as replete with vitality. The third strophe joins the theme of time to that of space, as the human march through centuries reaches into the present.

In the fourth strophe, the poet addresses directly the buildings around him that represent reality at the moment. He notes their nobly worn appearance and asks—again, rhetorically—the meaning of so much aimless meandering through centuries of haphazard development. The question is then answered in the final lines. The poet comes upon the center of the city, as four streets lead into the central square. The aim of humanity, the poet declares, is indeed the unity symbolized by the central point of collectivity.

The word "bella" (last line), translated here as "exquisite," alternated with two other possibilities in Guillén's original drafts for this poem. These words were "sacra" and "sagrada"—"sacred"—indicating that the center is indeed a holy place.[44] The final form of the poem is less suggestive of religiosity, but the attainment of unity is nonetheless an individual and collective goal, a "victory," in the poet's words.

Mandala symbolism, an ancient form of artistic expression, is fused with Guillén's own poetic imagery. While his geometrical images are less elaborate than those of the plastic arts, his symbolism of unity has much in common with the ancient images of the circle and square. In a letter dealing with this subject, the poet expresses himself as follows: "Quizás asimilé una difusa influencia. Total: que me he expresado así por una inclinación espontánea. Mucho mejor que ese sentimiento individual corresponda a un pasado milenario, a una tradición" ("Perhaps I assimilated a diffuse influence. At any rate, I have expressed myself thusly through a spontaneous inclination. It is much better that my individual sentiment should belong to a millenial past, to a tradition").[45] Let it suffice to state in summary that Guillén's poetic originality both reflects and enriches the archetypal validity of mandala symbolism. But a more consuming interest for the poet is the vision of poetry itself, the topic of the last section of this essay on *Cántico*.

VI *The Function of Poetry*

"Yo no sé qué es la poesía y . . . su definición general no me interesa" ("I do not know what poetry is, and a general definition does not interest me").[46] This declaration, taken from an inteview, may be interpreted to be somewhat mischievous and simultaneously quite serious. Poetry for Guillén is an integral part of life itself and, like life, is experience and process rather than dogmatic definition and formula. There are no poems in *Cántico* that deal with literary movements or schools of thought as such. While Guillén and his contemporaries during the 1920s were involved with the ideal of "pure" poetry, such aesthetic renovation is best seen in practice, not theory.

If Guillén is not preoccupied with preconceived notions of what poetry *is*, his view of what poetry *does* is quite another matter. He is vitally interested in the *function* of poetry in his own life and that of his anonymous friend, the reader. In the final dedication of *Cántico*, Guillén addresses first his friend Pedro Salinas, then the reader, who he hopes will be:

HOMBRE COMO NOSOTROS
AVIDO
DE COMPARTIR LA VIDA COMO FUENTE,
DE CONSUMAR LA PLENITUD DEL SER
EN LA FIEL PLENITUD DE LAS PALABRAS

(*AN*, 537)

A man,
eager as we
to share life as a fountain,
to consummate the fullness of being
in the ever-faithful plenitude of words.

An examination of the role of poetry as it emerges in *Cántico* will show that Guillén's vision of his art is, not surprisingly, quite similar to other aspects of life that he describes in poetry. The reality of the world is always of paramount importance in *Cántico*, and poetry captures the essence of reality for both the poet and his reader. To capture the essence of reality means in part to bring to light vital elements of our daily normalcy that might otherwise go unnoticed and unremarked. Finally, and perhaps most importantly in Guillén's view, the poet endows a given moment or event with permanence. Reality—life—is recorded by the poet, and the daily truths of life experience are preserved for the aesthetic collaboration of present and future readers.

The role of the poet as commentator is seen in the first poem of *Cántico*, "Beyond," wherein Guillén affirms his view of the primacy of external reality, noting that he as poet provides an "explanation" of the reality of the world, just as the "legend" of a monument clarifies its significance for those interested in it (*AN*, 28). Elsewhere, Guillén describes metaphorically the process of poetic creation and the recreation of reality in the poem, as well as the existential reality of the poem for the artist.[47]

Guillén's ideas on the function of poetry are developed in a single long poem, "Vida extrema" [Utmost Life]. Just as "Beyond" contains the poet's most thorough commentary on his vision of the world, "Utmost Life" is an exposition of Guillén's varied ideas on poetry that appear separately or individually in other poems. A study of the themes of "Utmost Life" will therefore summarize Guillén's aesthetic ideas in general. The poem is reduced considerably here from its original forty-five strophes; nevertheless, there are key verses in which the principal themes are concisely stated. Omissions are indicated by ellipses.

Guillén divides the poem into three sections, which can be labeled as prologue, narration, and epilogue. As the poem begins, the speaker, referred to somewhat impersonally at first as the "wanderer," enjoys a pleasant afternoon, but reflects on the transitoriness of the scene:

Hay mucha luz. La tarde está suspensa
Del hombre y su posible compañía.
Muy claro el transeúnte siente, piensa
Cómo a su amor la tarde se confía.

. . . .

¡Ay! Tiempo henchido de presente pasa,
Quedará atrás. La calle es fugitiva
Como el tiempo: futura tabla rasa.
¿Irá pasando todo a la deriva?

(*AN*, 398)

The day is brilliant. The afternoon depends
upon the man as its possible companion.[48]
The wanderer, feeling clear-headed, thinks
of how the afternoon relies on his love.

Ah! The fullness of the present passes,
it will be left behind. The street, like time,

is fleeting—a blank in the future.
Will all be left adrift [in the past]?

In these strophes from the prologue, Guillén presents the issue and the question that he will resolve in the rest of the poem. The opening lines contain an affirmation of the vital collaboration that necessarily exists between the poet and his environment. However, unlike the attitude seen in other poems, Guillén here appears to accord primacy to the poet rather than to nature alone. The pleasant scene "relies" on his affection for it, for reasons later developed at length. The second strophe adds another new element to Guillén's accustomed vision, this time regarding temporality. The speaker appreciates the moment for its fullness—a typical attitude in *Cántico*—but notes that the moment will be lost in the future. Guillén concludes the strophe (and the prologue) with a rhetorical question about the future that will become the main theme in the second part of the poem.

The second, main section of the work constitutes an essay in verse on the stages of the aesthetic process. Here Guillén describes the chain of poetic creation from virginal nature, to the words that form the poem, to the eventual reader. Initially, he continues the thought that the afternoon scene is as yet unfinished, for it has yet to become recreated as poetry:

Una metamorfosis necesita
Lo tan vivido pero no acabado,
Que está exigiendo la suprema cita:
Encarnación en su perenne estado.
. . . .

(*AN*, 399)

[This day], so fully lived but incomplete,
needs the transformation
that this supreme encounter demands:
the incarnation of its eternal state.

This transformation, which Guillén's friend and fellow poet Pedro Salinas appropriately calls "alchemy" (see note 18), depends upon the interaction—"supreme encounter"—of the world and the poet. The result of the encounter will be the permanent incarnation of the day in art.

Guillén continues this line of thought several strophes later, as he speaks lovingly of the words that will form the poem. To the mission of permanence realized in the poem, Guillén now adds the poetic function of light or illumination:

> Revelación de la palabra: cante,
> Remóntese, defina su concierto,
> Palpite lo más hondo en lo sonante,
> Su esencia alumbre lo ya nunca muerto.
>
> Más vida imponga así la vida viva
> Para siempre, vivaz hasta su extrema
> Concentración, incorruptible arriba
> Donde un coro entre lumbres no se quema.
> . . . .
>
> (*AN*, 400)
>
> The revelation of the word: may it sing,
> rise up and complete its harmony,
> may its most sonorous depths break forth,
> and may its essence brighten what will never die.
>
> May vital life thus impose more life
> forever, alive in its [most intense]
> concentration, [in] its lofty purity
> where, a chorus among flames, it cannot burn.

The word as light is applauded for its clarity and permanence, now that the scene is in the process of being recorded. The near litany of *life* in the second strophe indicates clearly the existential vitality that poetry holds for the artist. Guillén concludes the strophe with a Platonic overtone: the true life of the poem is mental, so the illumination that it provides is metaphysical, and therefore "pure" or "incorruptible" and cannot "burn." The poem is a concrete thing, but the enlightenment that it brings belongs to the life of the mind.

As the work continues, the poetic ideals of enlightenment and permanence become joined to the idea of the recreation of reality in art:

> El tiempo fugitivo no se escapa.
> Se colmó una conducta. Paz: es obra.
> El mar aquel, no un plano azul de mapa,
> ¡Cuánto oleaje en nuestra voz recobra!

Y es otro mar, es otra espuma nueva
Con un temblor ahora descubierto
Que arrebata al espíritu y le lleva
Por alta mar sin rumbo a fácil puerto.
. . . .

(*AN*, 401)

Fleeting time does not escape.
The act [of creation] has been fulfilled. Peace: the act is a work.
The sea, not the flat blue of a map,
recovers such a surge of waves in our voice!

And it is another sea, another foam
with a newly discovered quivering
which captures the spirit and carries it away
on the high seas, not to a docile port.

At this point the process of creation is complete in the form of a finished poem. The speaker feels strongly, of course, that the recreation of nature in poetry is revitalization as well as art. Thus, the sea appears in a fresh surge in the poem, quite unlike the dull reproduction that would typify a more prosaic rendering such as a map drawing—i.e., reproduction *without* revitalization.

An important shift of emphasis occurs in the above strophes regarding collaboration. The poet has ceased to speak of his interaction with nature, and turns his attention toward another form of collaboration, that which he now proposes to establish with the reader. He refers to recreation in "our" voice. The usage can be assumed not to be an editorial "we," since throughout the poem the speaker refers to himself in the first or third person. Furthermore, he speaks in the second strophe of a voyage of discovery, when he himself has already completed his artistic mission. Several strophes later the reader is mentioned again somewhat tentatively, then addressed directly:

He aquí. Late un ritmo. Se le escucha.
Ese comienzo en soledad pequeña
Ni quiere soledad ni aspira a lucha.
¡Ah! Con una atención probable sueña.
. . . .

Minutos en un tren, por alamedas,

Entre doctores no, sin duda en casa.
Allí, lector, donde entregarte puedas
A ese dios que a tu ánimo acompasa.

Entonces crearás otro universo
—Como si tú mismo lo hubieras concebido—
Gracias a quien estuvo tan inmerso
Dentro de su quehacer más atrevido.
. . . .

(*AN*, 403–4)

Here. A rhythm throbs. It is heard.
That beginning, in quiet solitude,
seeks neither seclusion nor struggle.
Ah! But it dreams of probable attention.

A few minutes on a train, in parks,
not among scholars, [but] of course at home.
There, reader, where you might devote yourself
to that god who will impregnate your spirit with song.

Then—as if you yourself had conceived it—
you will create another cosmos,
thanks to the man who was so immersed
in his most daring task.

The finished poem is now in the public domain, having left its creator, only to be created anew in the mind of the reader as its musicality strikes a respondent chord. The poet goes on to add that he hopes his work will find acceptance away from the "ivory tower" of strictly academic readers, and so he mentions trains, parks, and homes.

The attention of the reader will lead to recreation on his part. The suggestion in the second strophe that there is a "god" of poetry might initially appear to be something of an overstatement, but not if this line is interpreted within the larger context of the poem and Guillén's world in general. No one poem is a god, but poetry represents the principle of creation, which Guillén considers a divine force in human life.[49] The creation principle will permit the vitality of nature, reborn once in the poem, to be created yet another time through reader participation.

Continuing with the idea of recreation through the reader, Guillén becomes somewhat uncharacteristically personal. In the closing strophes of this main section, he declares that he himself will live on through his poetry, and thus gain a measure of immortality:

> Eso pide el gran Sí: tesón paciente
> Que no se rinda nunca al No más serio.
> Huelga la vanidad. Correctamente,
> El atentado contra el cementerio.
> . . . .
>
> En la palpitación, en el acento
> De esa cadencia para siempre dicha
> Quedará sin morir mi terco intento
> De siempre ser. Allí estará mi dicha.
>
> (*AN*, 404)

> The Great Affirmation asks this: patient tenacity,
> never surrendering to the most ominous Negation.
> [This is] not useless vanity, [but a] proper
> assault against the grave.
>
> In the palpitation, the intonation
> of that cadence, forever said,
> my stubborn intent to be forever
> will not die. My good fortune will be there.

The speaker has now come full circle from the attitude expressed at the beginning of the poem. The chain of creation that begins with nature and continues through the poet and reader accords a permanence to the poet that *he* would not have attained were it not for the poem. The initial interaction that caused nature to be preserved applies to the poet as well at his own level. The poetic stance is clearly in agreement with Guillén's positive vision of the world: affirmation triumphs over nihilism and despair, and art is a symbolic (and "proper") weapon against the annihilation of death. The words that Guillén chooses to describe the future repetition of the poem—"palpitation," "intonation," "cadence," "forever"—underscore the idea of vitality in the work.

The concluding section comprises a relatively brief summary that refers back to the previous themes. The speaker answers his initial rhetorical question about the day being lost in the past. The answer, of course, is that the day has been saved for posterity because of the artist:

Sí perdure el destello soberano
A cuyo hervor la tarde fue más ancha.
Refulja siempre el haz del aquel verano.
Hubo un testigo del azul sin mancha.
. . . .
(*AN*, 405)

Yes, may the noble beam survive,
for whose light the afternoon broadened.
May the rays of that summer shine always.
There was a witness to the flawless blue sky.

Here the parallel "salvations" of nature and the poet are joined in a mutual quest. The poet expresses the hope that his art, now seen again as light, will survive, and the day will continue to exist as will the testimony of the witness. In the brief epilogue, therefore, Guillén resolves the tensions established earlier in the text.[50] "Utmost Life" contains Guillén's ideas on the function of both art and the artist, with emphasis placed on the idea and goal of permanence. Permanence is also an ideal, one which joins in part the various principal themes of *Cántico,* as seen in the following general summary.

VII *Summary—The Transition to* Clamor

If the principal themes of *Cántico* are considered together, it becomes apparent that *transcendence* is the common denominator of the work as a whole, and self-realization is the most basic personal goal of the speaker throughout the collection. In the major themes studied in this chapter—external and internal reality, love, time and death, personal fulfillment and geometrical imagery, and the function of poetry—the poet's vision surpasses egocentricity and transcends specific time and place. The result is a poetry grounded in everyday reality, but which achieves universal validity and appeal through the exposition and affirmation of collective human values. That is perhaps the most meaningful "pure" poetry: art springing from normalcy, but divested of all anecdotal periphery so that its essential humanity is visible in transcendent clarity. The five hundred pages of *Cántico* constitute a monumental exaltation of the fulfillment that is possible in daily life.

Nevertheless, Guillén could not write *Cántico* forever. The poet devoted thirty years to his masterwork, then felt a need to explore new directions in his poetic expression. After publishing the second edition of *Cántico* in 1936, Guillén witnessed the international catastrophes of the Spanish Civil War and World War II, and suffered the personal tragedies of exile from his homeland (1938) and the death of his first wife, Germaine (1947). While the poet found in his adopted New England home the tranquillity to complete the 1945 and 1950 editions of *Cántico,* he also began to gravitate toward his second major collection, *Clamor: Tiempo de historia*.[51]

A hint of the committed voice that speaks in *Clamor* begins to sound as somewhat of a murmur in the postwar versions of *Cántico*. The tone of the poet is still overwhelmingly positive, but one senses at times an affirmation in spite of circumstances rather than because of them. Guillén felt, therefore, that it would be fruitless to continue *Cántico* when he had evolved away from it. This is not to imply that *Clamor* is a brusque departure from the joy of *Cántico*. As will be seen, there is much optimism in *Clamor,* and Guillén's third major work, *Homenaje,* is a resounding reaffirmation of *Cántico* that appeared in 1967. During the late 1940s, however, the poet felt that to persist with *Cántico* would be to fall into monotony. In his own words:

> Importa mucho,—me importa a mí—la continua coherencia de toda [la] obra. Pero . . . cada poema nace de modo singular y no en previsto de un programa. Cada libro aspira a su propia unidad, a su propio acento. Si así no fuera, *Aire nuestro* sería un monumento monótono. Y, me parece, no lo es.[52]

> The continued coherence of the entire work is very important to me. But each poem is born in a unique way, and not as part of a preordained program. Each book aspires to achieve its own unity, its own tone. If it were not so, *Our Air* would be a monotonous monument. And it seems to me that it is not.

The final poem of *Cántico,* "Cara a cara" [Face to Face], is a ten-page restatement of Guillén's convictions regarding his positive outlook. The poet begins with a quote from García Lorca, then lists a catalog of ills which might assault any individual, anywhere, at any time. But he firmly declares his intent not to despair, and *Cántico* ends with these words:

Yo soy merced a la hermosa
Revelación: este Globo.
Se redondea una gana
Sin ocasos y me arrojo
Con mi avidez hacia el orbe.
¡Lo mucho para lo poco!
Es el orbe quien convoca.
¡Tanta invitación le oigo!
El alma quiere acallar
Su potencia de sollozo.
No soy nadie, no soy nada,
Pero soy—con unos hombros
Que resisten y sostienen
Mientras se agrandan los ojos
Admirando cómo el mundo
Se tiende fresco al asombro.

(*AN*, 533)

I am, thanks to the glorious
revelation: this Globe.
An undimmed desire
is rounded out and I rush
headlong toward the orb.
The great for the small!
It is the orb that convokes [all].
I hear such an invitation from it!
The soul [then] wishes to silence
its potential for tears.
I am no one, I am nothing,
but I am—with shoulders
that withstand and sustain
while my eyes open wide,
admiring how the world
offers itself, ever-fresh, to wonder.

Several ideas from the beginning of *Cántico*, "Beyond," are repeated here in the conclusion. The work begins at dawn, and in "Face to Face," light is still a dominant factor. In the poet's vision, the natural world continues to be the primary and supreme reality in human life. The themes of symmetry and unity also appear in the image of the "Globe" and the "rounding out" of the poet's desire to assimilate his reality at the moment. Last, Guillén affirms once more his attitude of wonder and astonishment at the world around him, despite the negative forces that bear down on all sides. In his second work, *Clamor*, Guillén turns his eye, his optimism, and his pen to confront those forces directly.

CHAPTER 3

Clamor: *The Poetry of Commitment*

UNLIKE the long publication history of *Cántico, Clamor: Tiempo de historia* [Clamor: Time of History] appeared as three separately titled volumes published over a six-year period. Together, they are approximately the same length as *Cántico*. The three collections are now generally considered as a unit, which is of course what the poet intended. Nevertheless, there are clear thematic differences in the volumes that constitute *Clamor*, and therefore the three works will be studied individually in this chapter. Before the publication of these works collectively in *Our Air*, Guillén issued them as follows: *Clamor I: Maremágnum* [Sea of Confusion, 1957]; *Clamor II: . . . Que van a dar en la mar* [We Will End at the Sea, 1960]; *Clamor III: A la altura de las circunstancias* [To Rise to the Occasion, 1963].

The titles themselves are indicative of a shift in focus from *Cántico* to *Clamor*, but the change does not represent a radical or schismatic division in Guillén's poetry. The author's attitude continues to be fundamentally one of optimism and affirmation, and he never loses sight of his role as an artist. There is, however, a notable change in the areas of life that the poet chooses to address and describe. His shift of emphasis is especially apparent in the first volume of *Clamor, Sea of Confusion*.[1]

I *The Social Vision of* Sea of Confusion

Just as the word "clamor" can be translated "outcry," the title *Maremǵnum* might also be rendered into English as "pandemonium." The word describes well the chaos depicted in the collection. *Sea of Confusion* is used here because this translation seems to express Guillén's idea that contemporary civilization can be seen as drowning in its own political, social, and technological waste. The collection is Guillén's one book that can be reasonably characterized as social poetry, by and large.

Naturally enough, many themes first enunciated in *Cántico* reappear in *Sea of Confusion*. But they are now treated from the point of view of a very contemporary speaker, and subjects which are seen in *Cántico* as having transcendental and permanent value here become intrinsically and temporally a part of the twentieth century. Accordingly, this section will focus on contemporary civilization as Guillén portrays it. While a single, long poem discussed below summarizes much of the dominant attitude in *Sea of Confusion*, several related aspects of this book on modern life should be examined first.

The committed voice of a speaker who has civilization on his mind is perceived clearly when compared with the voice that dominates *Cántico*. It may be remembered that *Cántico* begins with a description of dawn, as the poet comes to waking consciousness:

(El alma vuelve al cuerpo,
Se dirige a los ojos
Y choca.)—¡Luz! Me invade
Todo mi ser. ¡Asombro!

(*AN*, 26)

(The soul returns to the body,
arrives at my eyes
with a shock.)—Light! It floods
my being with wonder.

This expressed feeling of closeness to nature and resultant permanence contrasts starkly with the point of view in the following untitled, aphoristic poem from *Sea of Confusion:*

Amanece en el cristal,
La Historia se desperezа,
Ya vivo entre el bien y el mal.

(*AN*, 659)

It dawns in the window—
History [awakens and] stretches—
I now live between good and evil.

This brief poem contains two statements that would not have been made by the speaker in *Cántico*. In these lines the protagonist awakens not to a primordial or even a temporal world, but to a social environment. History is not natural history but society and politics, and the speaker emphasizes its present importance to him with a capital letter.

Furthermore, the daily reawakening of the historical process brings with it a dichotomy which, though acknowledged in *Cántico,* would never form the basis of one's orientation toward daily life. Existential truth and value in *Cántico,* it is worth repeating, lie not exclusively in the individual (subject) or in his environment (object), but in the vital interaction between the two. In the above lines, the situation is obviously quite different. Ethical values and potential decisions now dominate the poet's consciousness. The dawn perceived through his window is not one which inspires thoughts about creation, but feelings of ethical stance and implicit commitment.

The upheaval of values in modern society is described in many ways. A notable example is a prose poem entitled "Los atracadores" [The Holdup Men]. The narration recounts an armed robbery in Boston, and undoubtedly appears in prose because of the decidedly unpoetic subject matter described. Perhaps the most remarkable aspect of the event is the interpretation by the poet, who views the thieves as middle-class Americans at work:

> Boston. Sábado por la mañana. Gran vestíbulo
> de gran hotel. Hilos de novelas se anudan con
> tanta corrección que no se advierten.
>
> Entre el despacho de flores y el de cigarrillos,
> entre los que observan poco y los que se van
> con calma, de repente irrumpe,
>
> Ágil, veloz, tajante, una cuadrilla. Se sitúan
> en sus puntos de eficacia los enmascarados. A la
> agresión multiplica la estupefacción.
>
> Ya el cajero entrega los miles de dólares de
> la semana. Nadie chista. Ya los atracadores
> huyen sobre cálculos de fuga.
>
> Huyen, huyen, huyen con sus Monedas y se
> precipitan hacia el Óptimo Fin los más desespe-
> radamente burgueses, los tan apresurados.

No se atienden a reglas, las violan. Con tal vigor
asumen las ambiciones de todos. ¡Dinero hacia
Vida Confortable!

(*AN*, 699)

Boston. Saturday morning. The grand lobby
of a great hotel. Threads of novels are tied together with
such propriety that they go unnoticed.

Between the flower and tobacco shops,
between those who observe little and those who leave
calmly, suddenly there bursts in,

nimble, quick and sharp, a gang. The masked men
efficiently take their places. The stupefaction
increases their aggression.

The cashier delivers the thousands of dollars of
the week. Not a word is said. The thieves
escape in their calculated flight.

The desperately bourgeois, hurried gangsters
flee, flee, flee with their Money
toward the Very Best Purpose.

They do not abide by the rules, but break them. With such
vigor they adopt the ambitions of us all: Money for
the Good Life!

The obvious but significant irony of this narration revolves around the notion that the robbers in their well-executed plot are following a definite work ethic in pursuing the American dream. The orderly scene at the hotel (a humorous comment on the New England concern with propriety) is disrupted by the precise maneuvers of the thieves, who break the common societal rules, the speaker states in the final strophe, but only because they are striving for what is normally associated with success in contemporary life. And the thieves pursue their careers with appropriate Yankee ingenuity and vigor. They typify a world without values, or with inverted values, in which traditional ethical or moral systems cease to function adequately but are not replaced by other meaningful values.[2]

Modern civilization brings with it modern technology. Guillén's attitude toward technology appears to be largely neutral or indifferent. Occasionally, however, he remarks on the lack of beauty and character in the contemporary creations of a technological society. It may be remembered that in the poem "Plaza mayor" [Main Square, *AN*, 473], from *Cántico,* humanity's wandering through history finds unity and purpose in the totality represented by the symmetrical, central square of an old city. Such grace is notably absent, however, in "Rascacielos" [Skyscraper], as the speaker gives his opinion of contemporary geometrical perfection in architecture:

> Sobre el compacto caserío
> Que dividen las paralelas
> De unas calles—sin corruptelas
> En quiebros curvos por el río
> Del azar—se levanta, frío
> Cálculo o fervor de intelecto,
> Otra ciudad: empuje recto,
> Que elevándose hacia el futuro
> Prefiere tajante el gran muro,
> Abstracto como su proyecto.
>
> (*AN*, 662)

> Above the compact houses
> that divide the parallel lines
> of the streets—without the corruption
> of bending curves by a river
> of chance—another city rises up,
> a cold calculation or intellectual fervor:
> an angular thrust which,
> rising up toward the future,
> prefers that the great wall be cutting,
> [as] abstract as its projection.

The building, like the future, seems to be under construction when viewed by the poet. This situation means that the building exists completely only in the minds of its creators, which is to say that it is removed from natural reality. The perceived attitude of cold abstraction dominates the poet's thought throughout the poem. Indeed, the idea of a technological reality apart from nature is repeated in almost every line of the poem: parallel lines, no curves of chance, cold calculation, intellectual fervor, angular thrust, rising up, cutting wall, abstract projection. This building is itself as alienated from nature as contemporary life is often portrayed to be. The irony of this particular poem is that the building in its present stage of development is an "abstraction" and thus in a sense "unreal," but when seen from a natural perspective it will continue to be somewhat unreal after its completion, standing in sterile geometric perfection, devoid of adventure or interesting qualities. As Guillén states in another short poem, "Epílogo" [Epilogue]:

—¿Y la tierra?—De avión
Murió.—¿Por qué ese final?
—Falta de imaginación.

(*AN*, 661)

—And the earth? It died of
an airplane.—And why that end?
—Lack of imagination.

While it might appear from the above poems that nature is pushed into the background in *Sea of Confusion,* such is not the case. However, nature is often used as the counterpoint to technological progress in order to underscore the poet's ironic vision of society. As in *Cántico,* the speaker in *Sea of Confusion* emphasizes the permanence of natural order, as opposed to the finite, monumental events of history. The difference in point of view from one work to the other is that in *Cántico* the attitude is fundamentally one of affirmation, but shifts to irony in *Sea of Confusion*. In "Barba con nido" [Beard with a Nest], Guillén describes a statue of St. James, the patron saint of Spain, in a conquering pose over a fallen enemy:

A los pies del caballo queda
Con su coraje aún, maltrecho,
Final fortuna de su rueda,
El moro español. Es un hecho
De historia. Contemplad. Santiago
Combate y remata el estrago
De aquel ejército vencido.
Pero en la barba, que no es poca,
De Santiago un ave coloca
—Paz y vida sin fin—su nido.

(*AN*, 650)

At the nadir of his wheel of fortune,
still with his mettle, battered,
at the feet of the horse
lies the Spanish Moor. It is

historical fact. Behold. St. James
combats and finishes off the remains
of that vanquished army.
But in the beard of St. James, which is no small thing,
a bird builds its nest—
Peace, and life everlasting.

In the first sentence of the poem, Guillén summarizes eight centuries of Moorish presence in Spain. From the cultural glory of the Caliphate, the peak of the historical "wheel of fortune," the Moor was defeated during the Christian reconquest. The poet takes dutiful note of the historical lesson as would a tourist at a national monument. His attention then centers on the beard of the allegorical statue. The beard is the traditional symbol of nobility and virility in medieval literature, and so the beard of St. James represents his historical significance as spiritual patron of the reconquest. And it is there, of course, that the speaker sees a manifestation of life that continues eternally, unconcerned with the historical event. The bird building its nest implies springtime, which in turn points to rebirth and regeneration in nature. Guillén uses the same image when speaking of a less saintly conqueror, Hernán Cortés. In "Los supremos" [The Supreme Ones], the poet describes a town square in Mexico, then concludes with these lines that reaffirm in his view the primacy of natural life:

¡Qué de pájaros
Dominando a todos cantan,
Últimos conquistadores,
Ay, Cortés, de Cuernavaca!

(*AN*, 657)

What [a flock of] birds
sing, dominating all,
the last conquerors,
ah, Cortés, of Cuernavaca!

The ironic tone that characterizes much of *Sea of Confusion* is nowhere more apparent than in the humorous and satirical poems in which Guillén comments on the modern world and on comical human shortcomings. The most notable satirical pieces are three- and four-line aphoristic poems that Guillén calls "Tréboles" [Clover Leaves]. There are seven groups of "Clover Leaves" in *Sea of Con-*

fusion, in which the author treats a variety of subjects in a generally lighthearted vein. As an observer of society, for example, he comments on political candidates:

—Los candidatos son dos.
—Nunca posible eminencia.
Buen mediocre nos dé Dios.

(*AN*, 642)

The candidates are two.
There is no possible eminence.
May God provide a good mediocrity.

In a "Clover Leaf" probably more comprehensible to American than Spanish readers, Guillén toys with advertising in the United States:

Tuya es la aurora, Jesús.
Mira cómo luce el sol
En un cielo de "orange-juice."

(*AN*, 646)

The dawn is yours, Jesus.
See how the sun shines
in a heaven of orange juice.

Guillén's wit is especially enjoyable when he speaks of love and of male-female encounters in humorous terms. He can be the recipient of his own satire, as when he finds himself drawn to a woman's noticeable cleavage:

La mirada de admiración
En ese tan visible escote
Cae como carta en buzón.

(*AN*, 635)

Into that low and visible neckline
a look of admiration
drops like a letter in a slot.

The poet also allows himself an occasional fantasy in print, commenting on a lady that he presumably admires from a distance:

"Oh vous que j'eusse aimée," pensé.
El minuto volaba tanto
Que procuré no perder pie.
—¡Todo es ya, potencia de encanto!

(*AN*, 649)

"Oh you that I might have loved," I thought.
The minute was flying by so quickly
that I tried not to lose my footing.
All is now potential enchantment!

A similar admiration takes him virtually to heaven's door:

¡Oh delicia del banquete!
He de hablar con esa dama.
No sé ni cómo se llama.
Se abre el Limbo, son las siete.

(*AN*, 654)

Ah, the delight of the banquet!
I must speak with that lady.
I don't even know her name.
Limbo is open, at the stroke of seven.

Despite his humor and satire, Guillén does not lose his basic conviction that loving relatedness is based on deep emotional feeling. In another "Clover Leaf," he summarizes his opinion of relationships that have no emotional foundation:

—Sin disputa es una . . . tal.
—Conozco peor palabra.
Qué insulto: "fácil." Total:
Sigue el cabrón a la cabra.

(*AN*, 665)

—Undoubtedly she is a . . . so and so.
—I know a worse word.
What an insult: "easy." To sum up:
the buck chases the nanny goat.

It is interesting to note that, in this poem, a casual sexual encounter reduces both participants to an animal level. There is no double standard of sexual conduct here, just as in Guillén's love poetry in general the partners are portrayed as equals. Woman and man uplift themselves together in a genuine loving relationship; here they participate in a mutual debasement. Debasement of one's sexuality is the theme of another serious but comically worded poem:

> ¡Ay, cuánto me desazonas,
> Mujer-galán de mujer!
> ¡Qué sino en burla nacer
> Con tal embrollo de hormonas!
>
> (*AN*, 641)

> Oh, how insipid you are to me,
> [burlesque parody] of a woman!
> What a ludicrous fate to be born
> with such a jumble of hormones!

The form and content of the short "Clover Leaf" poems show a new turn in Guillén's work, especially when compared with the more universal poetry of *Cántico*. But it is important to note that the poet's values do not really change from one work to the next. The poems of *Clamor* are on the whole far more anecdotal than those of *Cántico,* and because of the new anecdotal tendency the poet allows himself to become more personal in both his affirmative and negative statements about modern society. The rest of this section on *Sea of Confusion* is devoted to Guillén's most personal, most powerful, and most committed poetic statement on the fate of his homeland, ruled by an archetypal modern dictator for nearly forty years.

"Potencia de Pérez" [The Power of Pérez] is perhaps the quintessential poem of *Sea of Confusion*. In its fourteen pages, the author brings to the reader's attention his view of the cruel elements of a totalitarian government under which the individual exists primarily not for himself but for the state, in a Spenglerian prophecy come true. This perversion of natural order and freedom is intensified by the fact that the various branches—henchmen—of Pérez's government consummately *believe* in what they are doing. The repressive mentality of the dictatorship is sufficiently contagious so as to convince Pérez's civil, military, and clerical servants that they are in fact upholding the common good. The poem must have struck a sensitive nerve in Franco's government, for it was decided by his censors that, for the common good, *Sea of Confusion* (and, consequently, *Our Air*) should be banned in Spain, an act which later prompted Guillén to say that he never aspired to such an honor.[3]

The poem, reduced considerably here with omissions indicated by ellipses, begins at the end of a "victorious" civil war which brings Pérez to power. Perhaps the most notable aspect of the initial section is Pérez's feeling that his is the destiny of the country, and that his leadership is the divinely ordained will of God:

I

Hay ya tantos cadáveres
Sepultos o insepultos,
Casi vivientes en concentraciones
Mortales,
Hay tanto encarcelado y humillado
Bajo amontonamientos de injusticia,
Hay tanta patria reformada en tumba
Que puede proclamarse
La paz.
Culminó la Cruzada. ¡Viva el Jefe!
. . . .

Fajín hay de Cruzado fulgurante,
Ungido por la Gracia
Del Señor, que es el guía.

Guía a través de guerra
Tan cruelmente justa
Para lanzar un pueblo a su destino.

Destino tan insigne
Que excluye a muchedumbres de adversarios
Presos o bajo tierra:
No votan, no perturban. ¡Patria unánime!
. . . .

Oh Jefe, nunca solo: Dios te encubre.

. . . .

(*AN*, 572–73)

There are now so many
buried and unburied corpses,
almost living in mortal
concentrations,

there are so many jailed and humiliated
beneath heaped injustice,
there is so much homeland reformed in the grave
that peace
can be proclaimed.
The Crusade was accomplished. Long live the Chief!

There is the sash of the radiant Crusader,
anointed by the grace
of God, who is his guide.

[His] guide through such a
cruelly just war
to propel a nation to its destiny.

Such a glorious destiny
that it excludes the multitudes of adversaries
who are [now] imprisoned or beneath the soil.
They do not vote, they cause no disturbance. Unanimous homeland!

Oh Chief, never alone: God conceals you.

The images and meaning of the poem are self-evident, and do not require extensive commentary. Most notable in this first section of the poem is the association of Pérez's victory—and Pérez himself—with divine will and guidance. To borrow a cliché from American politics, Pérez does not wrap himself in the flag of the country, but in the vestments of religion. The perverse exploitation of the church by Pérez naturally has a parallel in Franco's rise to power in Spain. Guillén's ironic use of words such as "crusade" and "destiny" is drawn directly from the rhetoric of Franco's Falangist party. Also of relevance is the phrase that appears on Spanish coins minted during Franco's regime, which proclaims "CAUDILLO DE ESPAÑA POR LA GRACIA DE DIOS" ("leader of Spain by the grace of God"). This self-proclamation of the dictator that he is a divine-right ruler is used to strong effect by Guillén, especially in the second and third strophes of the poem.

In section 4, "Coro de policía" [Police Chorus], Guillén comments on the role of the police in a totalitarian state:

Correctos, brutales,
Sutiles, entramos,
Salimos, rivales

De lobos y gamos.

Por nuestras pistolas
Ilustres bergantes
Que viven de trolas
Son más elegantes.

Repertorio fino:
Engaño, tortura,
Muerte en el camino
Más que cárcel dura.

Tal es nuestra dicha
Que hasta el más honesto
Desde alguna ficha
Cae en nuestro cesto.

El Jefe ya sabe
Que es el Primer Cruzado
Mientras sea suave
La guarda a su lado.
. . . .

(*AN*, 577)

Proper, brutal,
subtle, we come,
we go, the rivals
of wolves and bucks.

By our pistols,
illustrious scoundrels
who live by deceit
become more elegant.

[Our] fine repertory:
falsehood, torture,
death on the road
rather than the hard prison.

Such is our fortune
that even the most honest man
can fall from a card file
into our garbage bin.

The Chief knows well

that he is the First Crusader
while the guard at his side
looks charming.

In these strophes, Guillén joins form and content by his use of a disconnected, staccato delivery and singsong rhyme. Just as the previous description of Pérez himself appears in free verse—that is, unstructured or formless in the context of Guillén's sculptured poetry—the police "chorus" chants a droll litany that reflects a lifeless and mechanical function in Pérez's society. The commentary satirizes the use of the police as a political force rather than an agency for the maintenance of order. As instruments of oppression, the dictator's henchmen interpret and use the law according to whim. Their own vision of the law and its application is especially clear in the third and fourth strophes, which appear to deal with judicial abuses and with the misuse of privileged information.

Perhaps the most hypocritical "chorus" is that of the clergy (section 7). Church and state are joined in a perverse union that underscores Pérez's association of his victory with divine will. The clerics chant as they march in a religious procession:

Humildes, reverentes,
Graves de dos en dos,
Conducimos las gentes
A Dios.

Recto poder profano,
Si a Dios no desafía,
Besa el anillo en mano
Del guía.

Dios gana nuestras luchas
Y aunque se llame Alá,
En todas nuestras huchas
Está.

La nación nos reserva
Su profundo gobierno,
Sin Dios caterva sierva
De infierno.

Las llamas al hereje
Le hacen señas: ven, ven.

Dios es con Nos el eje,
Amén.
. . . .

(*AN*, 581)

Humble, reverent,
majestic, two by two,
we lead the people
to God.

[All] righteous profane power,
if it does not defy God,
will kiss the ring on the hand
of the guide.

God wins our battles,
and even were he called Allah,
He is in all our
money chests.

The nation, without God
an enslaved mob of hell,
reserves for us its profound
government.

The flames [of hell] make signs
to the heretic: come, come.
God is, with Us, the axis.
Amen.

The clerics' hypocrisy provides the unifying factor in the above strophes. The ideal of divinity becomes a hollow icon in whose name church and state unite to insure the success of their mutual interest—power. In the second strophe, there is an appearance of tension between the government and the church, as the "chorus" proclaims that secular ("profane") power must pay homage to the symbol of authority held by the churchmen. Any discord is resolved in the fourth strophe, however, as the clerics declare their appreciation of Pérez's support in leading the masses along the appropriate path.

In the third strophe, Guillén underscores the clerics' concern with earthly power. The reference to a God who could as well be called Allah might be read in two ways. The poet could be referring to the fact that Christian churches have no monopoly on the abuse of power—though occurring under Pérez's guidance and manipulation, such abuse could transpire anywhere. Within the context of the poem, it is also quite likely that God is indeed quite irrelevant to the worldly, power-seeking clergy. Their lack of concern with genuine religiosity is also evident from the grammatically erroneous, mock use of Latin in the final strophe (which is not adequately translatable from Spanish to English), undoubtedly added by Guillén to indicate spiritually meaningless pomposity.

Following the characterization of the clergy comes a description of a parade on a national holiday, perhaps in commemoration of Pérez's victory. The description brings to mind countless newspaper photographs of military parades, remarkable only in their monotonous sameness. Pérez, resplendently dressed in his uniform, stands on a high balcony and observes the pomp of his marching soldiers.

After the parade, in the final section of the poem, Pérez retires to the palace of the monarchs of earlier ages. He has usurped the royal residence by force, and inhabits it as a further attempt to elevate himself to the level of royalty. The reference is certainly to the eighteenth-century El Pardo palace near Madrid, occupied by Franco after the Spanish Civil War. In his solitude, however, Pérez is assailed by a sense of his own vulgarity. Despite the palacial splendor, the pompous parades, and the self-generated glorification, he is, at bottom, nothing but Pérez. Were he an English-speaking dictator, he would look in a mirror and see only Joe Doakes:

> La ficción se disipa en soledades.
> A solas silencioso el tan nombrado
> No queda ni ante sí,
> Figura sin figura
> Si no se la proponen los espejos.
> Ni el esplendor antiguo del palacio
> Donde reside ahora y se repliega,
> Ya rey,
> Puede impedir que el hombre verdadero
> Se insinúe en la pausa,
> Y aparezca ese Pérez vergonzante
> Que embrollo y perifollo casi ocultan:
> Un Pérez, ay, terriblemente Pérez,
> El más terrible Pérez, que se llama
> Pérez y que lo es.
>
> . . . .

La tiranía avanza
Con excluyente fuerza
Sobre miles y miles de caídos
Por ley de asesinato,
Entre las muchedumbres
De boca amordazada.
Dogma, sangre, dinero.
Y Pérez, Pérez, Pérez.
. . . .

(*AN*, 584–85)

The [public] fiction dissipates into solitude.
Alone, silent, the acclaimed one
cannot remain [so exalted] even [in his own eyes]—
a featureless figure
unless presented [publicly] with [the artifice of] mirrors.
Not even the antique splendor of the palace
where he now resides and retreats,
as king,
can prevent the insinuation
of the true man in this [silent] pause,
nor the appearance of that shamefaced Pérez
whom lies and finery almost disguise:
a Pérez, oh, terribly Pérez,
the worst Pérez, he who is
Pérez, and nothing more.

The tyranny advances
with prohibitive force
over thousands and thousands of fallen,
by the law of murder,
among the crowds
with muzzled voices.
Dogma, blood, money.
And Pérez, Pérez, Pérez.

Alone, the pettiness of the man Pérez, not the leader by the Grace of God, rises to the surface. Away from the banners and carefully orchestrated public glorification of his regime, the highly polished super-ego of the dictator dissolves amid the fine surroundings that he has conquered for himself at the cost of liberty in the country and untold misery and loss of life. Guillén comments on the insanity of pointless conquest in the concluding lines of the poem:

Y el tirano conduce,
Cruel, solemnemente a ciegas listo,
Sin cesar infalible,
Su artilugio triunfal
A su quebrantamiento más penoso,
Más vano:
Explosión en el choque
—Y todos ya lo auguran—
Contra el vacío mismo. No hay futuro.
Se adivina latente
Clamor con un furor
Que llenará de espanto
La escena de la farsa:
Muertos y muertos, muertos.

(*AN*, 585)

And the tyrant,
cruel, solemnly and blindly prepared,
unceasingly infallible,
leads his triumphant scheme
to its most afflicted,
most vain rupture:
the explosion in the clash,
now augured by all,
with its very emptiness. There is no future.
There is foreseen, [still] latent,
a clamor with a rage
that will fill with terror
the scene of this farce:
the dead and the dead, the dead.

The poet concludes his essay in verse with a comment on the emotionally and morally unstable nature of the dictatorship, and hence its ever-increasing intolerance for whatever and whomever does not fall within the narrow confines of its world view. There can be no future, the poet seems to say, because there is no dialogue under such a government and therefore no civic evolution or progress. The ultimate and most ironic cruelty of this governmental blindness is that it is the innocent and the sincere dissenters, not the perpetrators, who will suffer the most disastrous consequences of the dictatorial neurosis.

As stated at the beginning of this discussion, "The Power of Pérez" is perhaps the most characteristic poem of *Sea of Confusion*; certainly it is broadly representative of the predominantly social content of the work, and in it, Guillén brings together various themes that he treats individually in other poems. The socially committed orientation of *Sea of Confusion* is its distinctive feature. While society and modern civilization are recurring themes in Guillén's poetry, in no other single work are these issues such dominant factors. In the poetic collection published immediately after *Sea of Confusion*, Guillén continues to write in the vein of "clamor." In the next collection, however, he turns his attention to an ancient and more universal theme, that of temporality and death.

II *Time, Loss, and Death in* We Will End at the Sea

The second volume of *Clamor* is something of a paradox. Thematically, *We Will End at the Sea* is Guillén's most unified collection; reflections on temporality and finitude thoroughly dominate the work. It can also be reasonably characterized as Guillén's most sorrowful poetry, since the poet meditates openly on the passage of time in his own life and future demise, and the personal feelings of loss resulting from the death of his first wife, Germaine. A paradox arises from the notion that love, though literally terminated by death, invests both man and woman with a transcendent and noble essence that goes beyond all immediate circumstances, even including one's own finitude.

For an overall understanding of Guillén's work and its evolution, it is important to note that the meditations of *We Will End at the Sea* are not qualitatively different from the feelings about death expressed in *Cántico*. The attitudes of acceptance and resultant existential authenticity characteristic of *Cántico* are seen equally clearly in *We Will End at the Sea*, and there is no need to repeat them here.[4] Guillén's ideas in the latter collection complement and extend those of *Cántico*, with the notable difference—not contradiction—that he is decidedly more personal in *We Will End at the Sea*. As mentioned in the preceding section, *Clamor* in general is far more personal and anecdotal than *Cántico*, and the poet's thoughts on death are no exception.

The intent in the following analysis of *We Will End at the Sea* is to delineate and explore Guillén's main tendencies in the collection.

His ideas revolve primarily around the themes of time, dying, and love as a symbolic transcendence of death. The poet also feels that art is to be esteemed for its permanence.

The title of the collection derives from one of the most powerful poetic works of the Spanish Middle Ages. The last important medieval Spanish poet, Jorge Manrique (1440?–1479), is known today principally for a poem of some five hundred lines which he composed in memory of his deceased father. The introductory section of the long elegy contains the following lines: "Nuestras vidas son los ríos / que van a dar en la mar, / que es el morir . . ." ("Our lives are the rivers / that will end at the sea / which is death"). Manrique's poem is a virtual compendium of medieval thought concerning temporality and death. Some salient ideas are of course no longer current, while others are as eternal as the theme itself.

By contrast, the speaker in *We Will End at the Sea* displays a thoroughly modern attitude, notable in part for its lack of an ordered, religious view of life and death. Nonetheless, Guillén draws on Manrique's image of the river in order to develop his own point of view, as seen in the following three "Clover Leaves":

. . . Y vuelve de pronto el frío,
Y está la noche más sola,
Y yo paso con el río.

(*AN*, 847)

And the cold suddenly returns,
and the night is more alone,
and I pass with the river.

Fiebre con escalofríos.
¿Un pérfido berbiquí
Trabaja dentro de mí?
Nuestras vidas son los ríos.

(*AN*, 853)

Fever and chills.
Is a treacherous drill
at work within me?
Our lives are the rivers.

Amanece. Siento frío.
Temprano llega el otoño.

Corre al mar, al mar mi río.

(*AN*, 846)

The dawn. I feel cold.
Autumn is arriving early.
My river runs, runs to the sea.

Although the aphoristic style of the "Clover Leaf" continues here from *Sea of Confusion,* these short poems now cease to be humorous. In *We Will End at the Sea* the poet uses this form to convey, at times telegraphically, notions and feelings best communicated by image and intuition rather than intellect. Because the poems depend largely on sensorial imagery for their impact, they require little commentary once the overall context of the poems is understood.

Having used the image of the flowing river with its traditional meaning, Guillén can also employ the river metaphor as part of his own contemporary view of time and death. In a short poem with a title that is ironically religious in tone, "Gracia temporal" [Temporal Grace], Guillén speaks of the flow of time that he accepts without the comfort of a religious ordering of the world:

De trascurrir no cesan los minutos,
Y el tiempo—que en el alma se acumula—
Acrece nuestro ser, así formado
—Mientras viva—por tiempo sustantivo.
Nada soy si no soy de esa corriente.

(*AN*, 793)

The minutes pass unceasingly,
and time—as it accumulates in the soul—
increases our being, [which is] thus formed
—while I live—by substantive time.
I belong to that current, or I am nothing.

The attitude in these lines is similar to that seen earlier in *Cántico*. Since death closes or terminates life, it gives life definition or completion, and must therefore be accepted as a prerequisite to fulfillment in life. The speaker realizes this existential fact and expresses his awareness and acceptance in terms of passing time. Just as Guillén affirms the necessity of *spatial* limits in life in order to define his intuitive center in the world, so too he realizes that *temporal* limits, although they are somewhat more philosophical and abstract, are a necessity in terms of his human delineation. The philosophical or intellectual acceptance of death, as well as the personal confrontation with one's impending fate, in no way diminishes the aura of mystery surrounding the dimly perceived event. For Guillén, personal assimilation of the reality of death does not make the prospect of dying any less terrifying as one confronts the unknown:

> Sí, ya me lo tragué. Ya tomo
> La vida lanzada a . . . morir.
> Pero, ¿cómo, Dios mío, cómo?
>
> (*AN*, 791)

> Yes, I swallowed it. I now see
> life as hurled toward . . . dying.
> But, how, my God, how?

On the other hand, the existential acceptance of death allows one to dispatch it as a central issue of individual consciousness, so that *life*—not death—can be approached with fulfillment in mind, not avoidance, since life must someday end. Despair, Guillén insists, is pointless and ultimately self-defeating:

> No, no hay menos primavera
> Frente a ese hombre que a solas
> No espera y se desespera.
>
> (*AN*, 791)

> No, there is no less springtime
> before that man who, alone,
> does not hope, and so despairs.

In this short poem, Guillén summarizes concisely a crucial if somewhat undeveloped attitude present in this collection and throughout his entire work. That is, that since personal knowledge of death is impossible to obtain, there is nothing to be gained from wallowing in the mental quagmire of one's necessary ignorance. Guillén's assessment of the subject could not be further removed from that of his older contemporary Unamuno, for example, who wrote continually about his religious doubts. But precisely because of the fact that Guillén does not wish to harp on this theme, it is rarely stated directly in his poetry, and he can therefore summarize his agnosticism in a three-line "Clover Leaf":

—¿Después del fin?—Sabe Dios qué
Será de mi total derrota.
—¿No temes, no esperas?—No sé.

(*AN*, 797)

—After the end?—[Only] God knows
what will become of my total demise.
—Do you not fear, or hope?—I know not.

One might say in summary that Guillén's philosophy of death emphasizes living, not dying, because the assimilation within himself of the reality of his own death frees him from its specter.

Since Guillén in *We Will End at the Sea* expresses a *living* philosophy about death, it is worthwhile to examine how the poet perceives life in the face of death—what he sees as the essence of human life that is so compelling as to prohibit the horrific aspects of death from overpowering his thoughts. In *We Will End at the Sea,* the quintessence of life is love. It is love that enables one to go beyond biological existence and achieve a spark of divinity. The poet develops this idea in "Luciérnaga" [Firefly]:

La noche aleja el prado,
Gris azul en lo negro. De pronto fulge un punto
Verde muy amarillo aligerado
Por tan rápida huída
Que apenas es ya vida
Cuando se desvanece, se enluta hacia un presunto
Casi aniquilamiento.
Desde la sombra mía yo presiento
La hermosura—que es luz—de aquel instante
Breve, feliz, mortal: relámpago de amante.

(*AN*, 800)

The night transports the meadow away,
blue-gray in the darkness. Suddenly a
lightened green-yellow point flashes
through such a rapid flight
that is just barely life
when it vanishes, goes into mourning in a presumed
near annihilation.
From my own shadow I divine
the beauty—the light—of that
brief, joyous, mortal instant: the lightning of a lover.

Stylistically, the poem is an excellent example of the symbolic use of natural objects in poetry. Guillén here speaks of life and love, not insects, and with the title he suggests to the reader the literal or physical plane on which he constructs his metaphorical commentary on the spiritual nature of love. One life, he says, is a flash of light in a context of darkness, a flash so brief as to be barely, momentarily visible before it sinks back into the blackness of night and nonbeing. The light emanates from the capacity for love, and so it is love that creates an illumined essence which extends beyond physical being.

Nowhere in Guillén's entire poetic work is love so clearly and poignantly identified with human essence as in the central section of *We Will End at the Sea*. In a thirty-eight-page section subtitled "In Memoriam" [In Remembrance], Guillén evokes the memory of his deceased wife, Germaine, who died at an early age in 1947. The poetry communicates the sad nostalgia of personal loss, in addition to the exaltation of love typical of Guillén's poetic outlook, combining the themes of death, loss, and nostalgia. He expresses openly their effects on his own life, which he reconstructs while in a tragic personal vacuum.

The poet deals in this section with intuition and feeling, and the brevity of the "Clover Leaf" form is particularly appropriate for the expression of his fleeting images. In two of these poems, he employs the image of a half-empty marriage bed to characterize the feeling of irrevocable loss:

Sobre esta misma almohada
Me acompañó su cabeza.
Sé ahora cómo empieza
La blancura de la nada.

(*AN*, 825)

On this same pillow
her head accompanied me.
I know now how the whiteness
of nothingness begins.

¡Ah!
Me afecta al despertar
El vacío de blancura

Que se extiende en tu lugar.

(*AN*, 814)

Oh!
Upon awakening, I am struck by
the empty whiteness
which spreads out in your place.

There is no arbitrary association of the color white with sadness in these poems, but rather a visual reinforcement of the sense of emptiness that comes from the loss of the partner. In another "Clover Leaf," the same image is used to indicate that the deceased lover continues to be an inspiration to the speaker through his memory:

El alba sobre la almohada.
Así empieza el nuevo día
Para que tu amor me invada.

(*AN*, 832)

Dawn on the pillow.
Thus the day begins,
so that your love might invade me.

The overpowering "invasion" of love in the form of a memory also reminds the speaker of both his past fulfillment and present emptiness:

Mocedad tan incompleta . . .
Pero me alumbró el amor.
Yo pude ser el planeta.

(*AN*, 815)

Such an incomplete youth . . .
But love illuminated me.
It let me be the world.

Noche a solas, vida vieja.
Ni uno soy en soledad.
(Yo viví, yo fui pareja.)

(*AN*, 815)

A night alone, an old life.
I am not [whole] even in solitude.

(I lived, I was a couple.)

¡Qué lejos, ayer de hoy!
Hondo ayer: dos fuimos uno.
Hoy no estás y yo no soy.

(*AN*, 834)

How distant, yesterday from today!
Profound yesterday: we two were one.
Today, you are not here, and I no longer am.

In these three poems, the partner is seen as the completion of the poet's personality, a fact remembered with mixed joy and mourning. In the first poem, he thinks back to their initial contact in youth, when the lover as soul figure expanded the speaker's inner horizons as a natural complement to himself. The memory of completion through love, however, is now cause for grief as the poet feels himself to be unfulfilled—a half that was once whole.

The idea of completion through the beloved is an important one for Guillén, considerably more than a romantic cliché. Due to the balance which Guillén perceives between outer reality and his own inner world, a change in his inward perception affects his vision of the outside world as well. This internal equilibrium is described much more amply in *Cántico* and *Homage* than in *Clamor*. Here too, however, the effect of the partner on the poet's external orientation is portrayed touchingly, as in the following key sonnet, "Entonces" [Then]:

Fue real, y por eso amor supremo,
Entonces, plena luz, no sólo ahora
Gracias a infiel y purificadora
Visión. Verdad exhumo. No la temo.

Entonces sí llegamos al extremo
De primaveras fértiles de flora
Que nos doraba el sol. Sin fin la dora.
Permanece el ardor. En él me quemo.

Ardimos. Nuestro fuego, cotidiano,
Duraba humildemente como brasa
De hogar sin presunción de gallardía.

Evidencia de espíritu en la mano:

Sólo reinaba lo que nunca pasa,
La Creación a luz nos sometía.

(*AN*, 831)

It was real then, and so it was supreme love
in the fullest light—not only now,
thanks to an inexact and purifying
vision. I exhume the truth, without fear.

Then did we [truly] reach the point
of a fertile springtime of flora,
gilded for us by the sun. Golden flora without end.
The ardor remains. In it I burn.

We were afire. Our daily flame
persisted humbly, the live coal
of a hearth without [exalted] pretensions of elegance.

The evidence of spirit [was] in hand:
only that which never passes reigned,
Creation delivered us to the light.

Despite the stylistic embellishments of this poem, the pronounced emphasis on *realism* between the lovers is reminiscent of the prevailing attitude in *Cántico*. Repeatedly throughout the sonnet, the poet disclaims any notions of exaggerated (and therefore unreal) romanticism by affirming the daily reality of the relationship between the partners. The concrete reality which they created through daily effort—"it was real then"—led to spiritual completion for both, symbolized here by the extended metaphors of flora and especially fire. Normalcy leading to fulfillment is a distinct characteristic of Guillén's love poetry in general, and the idea is dominant in this poem despite the present circumstances of the speaker.

Given the medieval derivation of the title and part of the content of *We Will End at the Sea*, it is interesting to note that the above sonnet contains an element of courtly love. The lover is "unavailable" to the poet in any literal sense, and yet her image continues to exert a vital inspiration in the present. (The most celebrated instance of courtly love in European literature is, of course, Dante's idealization of Beatrice after her supposed death in 1290.) On the other hand, the poem is very contemporary and singularly representative of Guillén in the insistence on ordinary reality that leads to universal significance. The idea of continuing inspiration is stated concisely in two "Clover Leaves":

> Ni te engañé ni me engaño.
> Mi vivir ya corrobora,
> Pleno, las frases de antaño,
> Más verdaderas ahora.
>
> (*AN*, 814)

> I deceived neither you nor myself.
> My living now confirms,
> fully, the phrases of long ago,
> more truthful now.

> Gentes que me son extrañas:
> Esas que me creen solo
> Sin ver que tú me acompañas.
>
> (*AN*, 835)

> People unknown to me:
> those who believe I am alone,
> who do not see that you accompany me.

Love here is a unique form of truth, *itself* a living entity, and as such it survives even those who create it. Just as in "Firefly" the essence of being is seen to be love, here love is an essence that the lovers create, and which then has being beyond them. This ideal reflects a fundamental continuity from *Cántico* to *Clamor*, despite the different perspectives of the two collections.

The transcendent nature of love in *We Will End at the Sea* is paralleled, in Guillén's view, by temporal transcendence through art. In "Ciervos sobre una pared" [Deer on a Wall], the poet comments on the prehistoric cave paintings at Lascaux, France. He removes himself somewhat from his subject—there is no first-person narrator—in order to reinforce stylistically the isolation of the animal figures frozen in time on the wall. Through art, however, these figures which represent living beings stubbornly persist, and spring to life before the poet. He studies the struggle of Art and Time, and remarks on the survival of art through the millenia:

> Emergen, se adelantan, vibran
> Sobre una pared de la cueva
> —A través de siglos y siglos

Profundizados en tiniebla
De inmóvil silencio recóndito
Que ni la Historia misma altera—
Los ciervos, los ciervos en fuga.
. . . .
Uno tras otro siguen juntos
Alzando siempre las cabezas
Adorablemente alargadas
Tras una vaguedad de meta.
Refrenado palpita el ímpetu
Que bosques y bosques desea.
Al perfil, otorgan, nervioso,
Aireación las cornamentas,
Y hasta se percibe el susurro
De las soledades inciertas.
Vibrando resaltan los ciervos.
En su vida sin muerte quedan.

(*AN*, 867)

They emerge, gallop and hurl themselves
on a wall of the cave
—deep in a fog
of still, dark silence
that not even History itself alters
through centuries and centuries—
the deer, the deer in flight.
They follow one another,
always raising high
their graceful, outstretched heads,
in pursuit of a vague goal.
The force [in them] which seeks
more and more forests
throbs in restraint [on the wall].
The antlers give airy movement
to the quivering profile,
and even the whisper
of uncertain solitude is heard.
The deer leap vibrantly.
In life without death they endure.

The immortalizing function of art links this poem thematically to "Utmost Life," the lengthy poem from *Cántico* in which the poet preserves the present moment and also a part of his own being through artistic creation. Beyond that common foundation, the two poems are quite different in both tone and thematic orientation. In "Utmost Life," the poet is openly personal as he looks toward the future. In "Deer on a Wall," the speaker *is* the future, as he gazes at the creation of an unknown kindred spirit, an anonymous artist who produced his primordial masterwork some one hundred to one hundred and fifty centuries ago.

Particularly noteworthy in this poetry about death is the intense emphasis that the speaker places on *life*. There is no mention of an individual creative artist, just as the speaker himself does not enter into the poem personally. But the poem itself palpitates with images of vitality. These are not animals statically frozen in time: they hurl themselves across the wall of the cave, they are in flight behind one another, raise their heads high in pursuit of an unseen goal, seek more and more forests in which to run, cause the air to rush through their antlers, persisting forever in their deathless orgy of motion. Like love in the preceding poem, the deer are the very emodiment of life itself.

Significantly, Guillén also underscores two common but remarkable aspects of prehistoric cave art: the figures are almost invariably depicted in profile—that is, in motion—and there is a striking absence of any embellishing scenery in the paintings—there are usually no trees, or even a groundline. In other words, there seems to be no attempt to represent anything but kinetic vitality. The speaker in the present is able to appreciate this vitality thanks to the creative act that has survived for thousands of years. Art, like love, is a transcendence of death. This may not be of overwhelming comfort to the individual, including the artist, who contemplates the specter of personal finitude. But art itself, the poet declares firmly, is an enduring force that will not pass away.

Given the crucial importance of the living entities of love and art in Guillén's poetic vision, it is possible to say in summary that *We Will End at the Sea* is a collection about death, but not about despair. There is stoic resignation, even anguish, in the work, but no ranting desperation—Guillén simply sees too much nobility in the human condition for dispirited capitulation in the face of death. It is this fundamentally affirmative outlook which enabled him to follow a book about death and loss with one that begins to reassert the exultant world view of *Cántico*.

III *The Transitional Poetry of* To Rise to the Occasion

As mentioned at the end of the preceding chapter, Guillén in his final stage of writing *Cántico* can be seen to be gravitating toward the committed point of view that dominates much of *Clamor*. An analogous situation exists in the third and final volume of *Clamor*, *A la altura de las circunstancias* [To Rise to the Occasion]. Here the poet quite clearly begins to shift away from the poetry that confronts negation, toward the mature and yet refreshingly jubilant poetry of *Homage*, a collection which comes full circle in its reaffirmation of the joy proclaimed in *Cántico*. The purpose in this section is to examine the way in which *To Rise to the Occasion* constitutes a coherent transition from *Clamor* to *Homage*.

To Rise to the Occasion is a transitional work primarily because, while the poet maintains the somewhat anecdotal qualities typical of *Clamor*, he sees in ordinary reality a universal affirmation of the human condition consistently asserted in *Cántico*. In the present work he depicts humanity in simple, elemental, daily terms, but plainly with the intent of affirming what is good and intrinsically noble in humanity, despite the occasional intrusion of negative circumstances. As Guillén stated in an interview:

> No es posible abandonarse al apocalipsis, al derrotismo, a una final anulación. La vida, la continuidad de la vida tienen que afirmarse a través de todas esas experiencias y dificultades. Por eso, aquí, en este libro se presenta más bien la condición general del hombre, porque la realización es la meta a la que todos nuestros esfuerzos deben tender. Nosotros no somos más que una tentativa hacia una plenitud propiamente humana.[5]

> It is not possible to abandon oneself to the Apocalypse, to defeatism, to a final annihilation. Life and the continuity of life must be affirmed through all these experiences and difficulties. For that reason, here in this book the general condition of man is presented, because man's self-realization is the goal toward which we should reach out with all our vigor. We are nothing more than an attempt at a peculiarly human plenitude.

The "general condition" that the poet describes tends more toward fulfillment rather than failure. Using his own titles as metaphors, he affirms human success in a particularly relevant "Clover Leaf" entitled "Domingo" [Sunday]:

"Es día del Señor.
Suene música sagrada.
Cántico sobre clamor"

(*AN*, 1007)

"It is the day of the Lord.
Let sacred music sound.
Canticle above clamor,"

A striking example of Guillén's positive vision of humanity is a poem about Anne Frank, appropriately entitled "La afirmación humana" [Human Affirmation]. In order to appreciate Guillén's point of view in *To Rise to the Occasion,* the poem might be compared with "The Power of Pérez," from *Sea of Confusion*. In that lengthy poem, emphasis is placed on the inhumanity of a totalitarian regime and the misery it causes. In the present work, however, the poet considers an equally horrendous situation, but focuses his attention on the hope that can be derived from an individual act of compassion in the face of adversity:

En torno el crimen absoluto. Vulgo,
El vulgo más feroz.
En un delirio de vulgaridad
Que llega a ser demente,
Se embriaga con sangre,
La sangre de Jesús.
Y cubre a los osarios
Una vergüenza universal: a todos,
A todos nos sonroja.
¿Quién, tan extenso el crimen,
No sería culpable?

La noche sufre de inocencia oculta.

Y en esa noche tú, por ti alborada,
A un cielo con sus pájaros tan próxima,
A pesar del terror y del ahogo,
Sin libertad ni anchura,
Amas, inventas, creces
En ámbito de pánico
Que detener no logra tus esfuerzos
Tan enérgicamente diminutos
De afirmación humana:

Con tu pueblo tu espíritu
—Y el porvenir de todos.

(*AN*, 953)

On every side, the absolute crime. Vulgarity,
the fiercest [mass] vulgarity
in a vulgar delirium
turned lunacy,
the mass becomes drunk with blood,
the blood of Jesus.
A universal shame
covers the ossuary as all,
all of us grimace.
So extensive a crime—
who could not be guilty?

The night suffers from hidden innocence.

And that night, dawn because of you,
so close [to being] a sky with birds
in spite of the terror and oppression,
you, without liberty or [freedom of movement],
you love, you invent, you grow
within the surrounding panic
that your spirit, so energetically tiny
in human affirmation,
does not succeed in detaining:
with your people your spirit,
and the future of us all.

In the first strophe, the poet remarks on the particularly perverse nature of the persecutions of World War II, inquiring rhetorically if all humanity does not somehow share culpability in the enormity of the crime. The message of the poem, however, appears in the second strophe, as the speaker turns his attention to an act of resistance and heroism in the face of overwhelming forces. The affirmative irony in Guillén's focus rests on the fact that an individual act was ultimately powerless against the war machine. Nonetheless, the poet concentrates on the human dignity and spirit implicit in the undaunted courage of Anne Frank and those around her. His concluding statement provides an answer to the earlier rhetorical question. If all must share in the collective guilt of persecution, all may derive hope and collective affirmation from the humble yet noble actions of a few. Guillén here does not perceive or expect a superhuman accomplishment but an attempt at the realization of the best efforts that one's humanity allows. That is the underlying theme of this poem, and of the collection as a whole.

The poet also deals with the goal of the realization of one's individual human potential in poems that are perhaps not dramatic, but important for an understanding of the attitude which characterizes the work. A short "Clover Leaf" sums up much of the poet's philosophy as expressed in the collection:

Negrura, luz, un respiro,
Trabajo, dolor, amor.
Ser hombre es lo que yo admiro.

(*AN*, 1006)

Darkness, light, breath,
work, pain, love.
Being man is what I admire.

Also in *To Rise to the Occasion*, Guillén begins to return to the salient idea of *Cántico* that each individual is an integral part of nature, and should accept and cultivate an existential relationship with the outside world. A quintessentially important aspect of being *human* is the realization that one is part of a vastly greater *whole*, as the poet states in the following two poems:

Noche perfecta sin un ruido
Que raye el perfecto silencio.
En Creación estoy sumido

(*AN*, 984)

Perfect night without a sound
to scar the perfect silence.
I am swallowed up in Creation.

Abril, domingo, mañana,
Vaivén de ensueño a sopor,
Fuerte luz en la ventana.
¿Yo? Más: el mundo exterior.

(*AN*, 980)

April, Sunday, morning,
a wavering from dreams to drowsiness,

bright light in the window.
Myself? And more: the world beyond.

The poet is a part of nature, but the majesty of the world is infinitely superior to him. This is another central thought from *Cántico* that all but vanishes in the first two volumes of *Clamor* due to the specific preoccupations of those collections. In *To Rise to the Occasion*, however, the idea appears again, as in the two short poems above. Another characteristic example is "Sierra" [Mountain Range], in which the poet admires the imposing beauty of the mountains around him:

Un sol de tiempo aterido
Pone en desnudo relieve
La sierra, que nos conmueve
Sin caricias al sentido.
El material, tan buído,
Sólo a un escultor sujeto,
Resalta y persiste, neto,
Modelado siempre a mano.
Musculatura de hermano
Mayor: impone respeto.

(*AN*, 1005)

The sun, stiff from the cold,
places the mountains in naked
relief, which touches us
without caressing the senses.
The stuff [of the mountain], so pointed,
stands out and endures, cleanly,
always modeled by hand,
subject only to a sculptor.
The muscular structure of a
big brother: it imposes respect.

In the first four lines (first sentence) of the poem, the speaker indicates that he is describing an attitude or frame of mind. He states that the mountains do not directly affect the senses—they are admired from a distance—so the impression they make is more mental than sensuous. The poet then turns his attention to the sculptured appearance of the peaks, despite their jagged crests and projections. This middle sentence of the poem is somewhat ambiguous, perhaps intentionally. The sculptor may be a divine master builder—God—or the earth itself may cause its own natural formations, which would invest the poem with a vaguely pantheistic tone. As usual, Guillén does not delve into questions that he cannot answer—he is content to imply that the natural world beyond him is enough to inspire thoughts of divinity. The poem concludes, then, with an affirmation of the overwhelming presence of the mountains in their towering majesty. Nature herself provides an affirmation of being in a manner strongly reminiscent of the poetic world view in *Cántico*.

In summary, it may be said that *Clamor* begins in war and ends in peace. The first volume, *Sea of Confusion*, provides a commentary on the modern world in upheaval. From social concerns, Guillén turns to perhaps his most touching and intensely personal poetry in *We Will End at the Sea*. In retrospect, this internal evolution from the social to the personal seems natural and even expected, as the poet turns away from the cares of the world to confront his own mortality. Having done so, it again seems natural for the poet to have completed his own evolution by transcending his preoccupation with death and returning joyously to the optimism of his earlier poetry. This he does in *To Rise to the Occasion*. If the circumstances of many poems appear to be somewhat more mundane and ordinary than those of *Cántico*, perhaps it is because the poet who has witnessed war and contemplated death now finds significance enough in the simplest daily experience, in just being a man, as he puts it.

In *To Rise to the Occasion*, then, Guillén puts *Clamor* aside. If Guillén had never written another line of poetry, his readers would almost certainly be unanimous in the judgment that in *To Rise to the Occasion* he reaffirms the ideals of *Cántico*. Such a collective opinion has not been needed, however, for the poet himself provides a ringing echo of his celebrated existential joy in a third major work, *Homage*, both a reaffirmation of the vision of *Cántico* and an exploration of new poetic themes.

CHAPTER 4

Homage, And Other Poems: *The Poetry of Reaffirmation*

WITH the publication of his third major collection, Guillén reaffirms values which are evident from his earliest poetic efforts in the 1920s. In *Homenaje: Reunión de vidas* [Homage: A Gathering of Lives], the poet introduces some new themes in his poetry, but the fundamental tone of joyous affirmation that characterizes the work almost in its entirety is vividly reminiscent of *Cántico*. This transcendence of the preoccupations that typify much of *Clamor* justifies the opinion of critics that *Homage* completes the circle of Guillén's poetic evolution.[1]

Two areas of thought that are truly distinctive in *Homage* are found in poems wherein Guillén deals with Eros and with metapoetry. While there are naturally many other themes in this lengthy volume, poems treating eroticism and poetic theory appear to dominate the collection, and will be examined in the following two sections. A third section in this chapter is devoted to Guillén's most recent collection, *Y otros poemas* [And Other Poems], which can be considered as a continuation of the tone and point of view of *Homage*.

I *Eros: The Symbolic Foundation of* Homage

It is interesting to note, on the second page of *Homage*, the primary dates of composition: from 1949 to 1966. These dates mean that, while he was writing and publishing the three volumes of *Clamor*, Guillén was simultaneously preparing his own rebuttal to that work. This fact in itself says much about the essential coherence and unity of vision in Guillén's poetry. The move away from *Cántico* had been quite conscious and premeditated, and the reaffirmation of its ideals was in progress at the same time as the poetry of commitment.

Since *Homage* is a reaffirmation of the spirit of *Cántico*, it is not surprising that love and an erotic vision of life should form the basis of the collection. In comparison with the fervent exaltation of love in all its facets that characterizes *Cántico*, the poet's treatment of the theme in *Homage* becomes more intimately joined to his inward vision and resultant emotional orientation toward the outside world. While there is less overt passion in *Homage* than in *Cántico*, the ideal of self-realization and transformation through love receives perhaps greater emphasis. The following commentary on Eros in *Homage* centers on three modes that Guillén favors: the spiritualization of love, the inner illumination derived from the feminine image, and the manner in which the image of woman determines in part the poet's vision of external reality.

As is the case with Guillén's love poetry in other collections, the erotic outlook in *Homage* is emotional and even sensuous without necessarily being sexual. Love is an attitude as much as an act, and so Guillén's sensitivity to Eros—feeling—appears in many poems that deal with topics other than lovemaking. Naturally enough, however, the erotic attitude of the poet emerges most clearly in his descriptions of love between man and woman. As in *Cántico*, love in *Homage* is idealized for its intrinsic value of relatedness, and because it opens the individual to contact with his inner self. The importance of this seemingly uncomplicated attitude cannot be exaggerated in any discussion of Guillén's love poetry. Eros—emotional, carnal, or both—is of paramount significance because it relates him to his own soul as he perceives it. The possibility of reaching the spirit through the flesh is a familiar theme from *Cántico* that all but vanishes in *Clamor*, then reappears vividly in *Homage*. Guillén describes the mutual fulfillment of lovers' spirit in "Divinamente" [Divinely]:

—Las bodas.
Gocémonos, amado.

—Con tu mirar me invades.
Y te invado.
Te invado

Yo todas,
Todas tus soledades.

(El alma no se sacia.)

Mutuamente en estado
De gracia,
Gocémonos.
Sagrado.

(El cuerpo al alma sacia.)

Paraíso inauguras
Con todas,
Todas tus hermosuras.

Gocémonos.
Las bodas.

(*AN*, 1129)

—The wedding.
Let us enjoy, my love.

—Your gaze invades me.
And I you.
I invade
all,
all your solitudes.

(The soul is not fulfilled.)

Together in a state
of grace,
let us enjoy.
Sacred.

(The body fulfills the soul.)

You unveil paradise
with all,
all your beauties.

Let us enjoy.
The wedding.

The most salient aspect of this poem is its quasi-religious tone, beginning with the title. The opening lines expand the significance of the title by establishing the double meaning of a physical-spiritual relationship. For readers of Spanish, the initial strophe is reminiscent of St. John of the Cross, while the idea of the wedding itself has both literal and symbolic connotations. Two beings merge into one in the flesh, while the souls are united in the "divine union" of masculine and feminine frequently symbolized in mystic literature. The second strophe continues the idea of each partner flowing into the other, which the poet calls an "invasion" of love.

The parenthetical comment that interrupts the lovers' dialogue is indicative of Guillén's tendency to find transcendent meaning that is contiguous to specific, concrete circumstances. Thus, after the remark that the soul is not fulfilled, the poem becomes more sensual and carnal in tone, and its language begins to resemble the eroticism of the Song of Songs. Emotional self-realization is still the poet's theme, but it is grounded in experience rather than abstract imagination. The resultant paradisiacal situation (lines 14–16) is the mutual creation of the couple, based on their specific labor of love. The poem is therefore rooted in a concrete situation that exists for the partners, but the poet's principal theme is emotional self-realization. This is a typical poetic stance in the love poetry of *Homage*, in which loving encounters are exalted for their potential in the quest for individual and mutual fulfillment.

There is another facet of the erotic poetry of *Homage* that is less direct and more symbolic in nature: that is the vital image of woman as she appears to the poet in his solitude, or, conversely, the manner in which he transforms the real partner into a soul figure. The poet occasionally refers to the assimilation of the beloved within his own soul as he perceives it, which is to say that the vital image is itself a means of self-realization. This image of woman, whether in the flesh or glimpsed internally with the mind's eye, is the key that admits the poet to the emotional world behind his masculine consciousness. Guillén's vision of the female partner as soul figure is in essential agreement with the symbolism and theory of the "anima" archetype expounded in Jungian psychology. The term "anima" means "soul," and Jung employs the concept of the anima figure to elucidate the manner in which the image of woman puts man in touch with the emotional component of his personality.[2]

The anima image therefore symbolizes the deepest emotional reality in man's personality. The image of woman is not merely a literary device or metaphor. It is, rather, the complement of male consciousness, and he must cultivate the inner reality of the anima if he is to realize his own emotional fulfillment. By seeing the feminine image in *Homage* as the transcendent anima figure, we can appreciate its importance as the necessary complement of the masculine mind. When the individual man is able to relate to the feminine image, it appears to him as a form of illumination from within himself, although symbolized concretely via the woman he loves. Guillén describes this inner illumination in poem number 6 from a series entitled "Amor a Silvia" [Love of Sylvia]:

> Amistad. Y después, ternura. Luego,
> Una atracción. Existe más la boca.
> Habla. Calla. Me place, sí, me entrego.
> Un alma muy concreta me convoca.
> Me ilumina el amor, ya no soy ciego.
>
> (*AN*, 1326)

> Friendship. And then, tenderness. Later,
> an attraction. There are lips, as well.
> They speak. They are silent. Yes, I am pleased, I surrender.
> A [real and] concrete soul summons me.
> Love illumines, I am no longer blind.

Here the poet succinctly narrates the development of a loving relationship grounded in daily experience. The initial reference to a dialogue of the couple indicates here as elsewhere an attitude of equality between the partners—they complement each other, but come to their meeting as equals, so neither is merely an appendage of the other. The situation is ordinary enough, and the poet does not need hyperbolic language to describe the realization of the couple's love. The element of reality is notable in line 4, in which the poet affirms that the experience of "soul" is specific and concrete. Love is a reality that illuminates the poet and expands his inner horizons. Lack of love would be tantamount to blindness, he declares, but love has delivered him from any such personal limitations.

An important aspect of the concept of love in *Homage* is that the inner illumination derived from the partner as soul figure effects the *outward* vision of the poet just as it expands his inner perception. To see the world erotically is to view objective reality with consciousness shaped by the image of the beloved. This idea is traditional enough, especially if it is simplified somewhat to the idea of being influenced by love. The implications of an erotic vision, however, extend beyond literary convention. Eros means approaching the world *itself* as an object of love, rather than an object of exploitation—a mine of symbolic meaning, rather than a source of material wealth. When applied to the world at large, erotic relatedness is essentially an ecological view of life, because relation is all-inclusive and the world is seen in terms of unity and wholeness, rather than abstraction and division. While material exploitation of the world necessarily implies separation and division, the erotic approach sees the essential oneness of life. Guillén notes this unity in "Entre" [Between]:

> Entre silencios
> La voz.
> Entre mis dedos
> Tus labios.
> Entre reflejos
> El sol.
>
> (*AN*, 1311)

> Between silences
> the voice.
> Between my fingers
> your lips.
> Between reflections
> the sun.

Especially noteworthy in this poem is the contiguous relationship that exists between the lovers and nature. The sense of oneness that joins the lovers to outer reality characterizes many love poems from *Cántico*, and in the reaffirmation of *Homage* the feeling of relatedness is the same.

"Caza" [Hunt] is another poem in which Eros draws the speaker to the world. As is typically the case in *Homage*, the poem recalls many affirmations of reality in *Cántico*, in that the world itself is a seductive force attracting the poet. The unique feature of "Hunt" is the presence of the loving partner who helps to make the world so attractive:

> A caza de la dicha salimos fatalmente
> Si nos dejan los otros: hambre, dolor, conflicto.
> Nada más verdadero que el corazón adicto
> Con esperanza al rayo de sol que dice: Vente.
>
> (*AN*, 1152)

> In pursuit of joy we sally forth fatefully
> if the other [forces] permit: hunger, pain, conflict.

> There is nothing more real than the devoted heart
> hoping for a ray of sun to summon: come hither.

Drawn by the light and clarity of the world, the speaker affirms his basic optimism in spite of negative forces working against him and his companion. The declaration of lines 3–4 give the poem an overall affirmative tone: love is the ultimate truth in life, and, along with the world itself, dominates despite negativity and nihilism. The speaker approaches the world objectively, realizing its imperfections, but that does not prevent him from seeing his life and his world as an object of love. The spiritualization of love and the internalization of the beloved's vital image affect the world view and artistic consciousness of the poet, and infuse in him an erotic outlook toward both his life and his work. Eros is crucial in *Homage* since it is indeed a "godly" force that shapes the poet's vision, and hence his orientation toward the microcosmic world within himself and external reality beyond him.

II *The Concept of Metapoetry*

If the world is an object of love in Guillén's view, it is also an unfathomable source of raw material that awaits transformation in poetry. In *Homage,* Guillén writes more than in other collections about the nature of the aesthetic process itself. Poems concerning poetic creation—that is, metapoetry—constitute a major theme in the work. The metapoetics of *Homage* have been examined in several penetrating critical studies.[3] Guillén's concern with the idea of literature is readily apparent in the first section of *Homage,* aptly subtitled *Al margen* [In the Margin]. In slightly over one hundred pages, he presents numerous glosses or commentaries—marginalia—reflecting upon past literary works. The works selected for this poetic commentary are worldwide, beginning appropriately with Genesis, and ending, not too surprisingly, with *Cántico*. Guillén's approach to these works is that of a subjective but perceptive reader. Just as the poet in *Cántico* perceives the transcendent essence of daily reality, the poetic commentator in *Homage* describes the essence of literary works from his own point of view.

After establishing his theoretical interest in literature in the initial section of *Homage,* Guillén moves on to speculation about the nature of poetry and the aesthetic process. "Enlightenment" and "communication" are the words which perhaps best describe the poet's attitude as it emerges throughout the work. The delicate relationship between poetry, understanding, and language—light and expression—is visible in "Candelabro" [Candelabrum], as Guillén states concisely the aesthetic point of view espoused in *Homage:*

Surge y se yergue, solo,
Sin romper el silencio de lo oscuro,

Un sonido con forma: "candelabro."
Apenas me ilumina vaga plata
Como la nebulosa en una noche
De inmensidad visible.

Pronuncio: "candelabro,"
Y se esboza, se afirma hacia su estable
Pesadumbre. Columbro: candelabro.

¿Adónde voy? Me esfuerzo,
Desde esta orilla torpe de un insomnio
Reducido a tiniebla,
En convivir, en dialogar ahora
Con algo que a su modo acompañándome
Ya está fuera de mí.

"Te necesito, mundo."

La palabra y su puente
Me llevan de verdad a la otra orilla.
A través de lo oscuro
Ayúdame, mi amigo, candelabro.

(*AN*, 1297)

Without breaking the silence of the darkness
it springs forth and rises up, alone,
a sound with form: "candelabrum."
[The sound] barely illuminates indistinct silver,
like the nebula on a night
of visible immensity.

I say "candelabrum,"
and it becomes sketched, then steady, toward its stable
weight. I glimpse; candelabrum.

Where am I [now] going? From this awkward
shore of insomnia
become uncertainty, I now strive
to coexist, to converse
with something outside myself
that accompanies me in its way.

"I need you, world."

The word and its bridge

truly take me to the other shore.
Help me through the darkness,
my friend, candelabrum.

The entire poem offers a commentary on the symbolism of light implied in the title, "Candelabrum." In keeping with the intimate tone that Guillén maintains throughout most of *Homage*, he concentrates here on the *personal* illumination that is part of the aesthetic process. Departing from the more or less traditional literary notion that the poet's role is to clarify the unconsciousness of nature, Guillén develops the thought that he expands his own horizons and consciousness as a result of his immersion in the waters of artistic creation.

In order to develop fully the idea of personal illumination through creativity, Guillén posits a metaphorical—and poetically real—relationship between language and light. This is the thought of the first strophe, in which the symbolic light of the candelabrum is seen as the result of the poet's fixation of his own consciousness and intellect. By stating that the "sound" of the word illuminates a surrounding darkness, he establishes the metaphor of an inner light of creativity that glows within himself. The same idea of language and resultant light is continued in the second strophe, as the candelabrum assumes a more tangible form, perhaps through the "mind's eye" of the poet.

In the third strophe, Guillén turns his attention to the transformation process within himself as he studies the candelabrum. The "shore of insomnia" implies both unconsciousness and a point of departure—the poet seems to state that he is in a condition of relative darkness, but about to leave this obscurity and embark on a voyage of poetic discovery. He accomplishes this goal by means of a vital dialogue with something that lies beyond him—in this case the candelabrum as representative of another dimension of reality. While this "other" reality can be seen as that of the everyday world, its importance in the poem is paramount, because the candelabrum draws the poet out of himself, thereby providing the possibility of self-transcendence and accompanying inner growth. As is usually the case in Guillén's work, the outside world is absolutely essential for the self-realization of the individual, as self-realization here is expressed in terms of poetic creation.

The poet emphasizes the importance of the outside world in the line that follows. By placing the statement, "I need you, world," in quotation marks, Guillén reinforces the idea of a dialogue with external reality that draws him beyond himself and thus toward expanded awareness. This attitude is in contrast with—though not opposed to—the aesthetic notion that nature needs the artist for the achievement of self-consciousness. Here, Guillén reverses the complementary relationship by affirming that reality contributes to his own expansion of consciousness by providing contact with that which is new or different to him.

The two themes of light and expanded consciousness are joined in the final strophe. By "crossing" a bridge from one shore to another, the poet states in effect that he moves from one level of consciousness—relative darkness—to another level of relative light. He thus transcends himself, leaving behind one boundary (shore) and moving to another perspective. He accomplishes this act by focusing his intuition and intellect on an object from external reality that helps him to rise above the previous level of consciousness. It is particularly appropriate that Guillén should employ the symbolism of light to describe the process of expanding consciousness, which he characterizes as internal illumination derived from the reality of the world beyond himself.

Naturally enough, Guillén sees poetry as being more than self-illumination, in *Homage* as well as in other collections. A consummately important aspect of artistic creation is communication with the reader. In the reader, the light of creativity shines with special intensity, for the poem is recreated in the reader, acquiring the added light of the reader's thought. Guillén comments on this poetic bridge of light in "Tentativa de colaboración" [Attempt at Collaboration]:

Sobre el silencio nocturno
Se levantan, se suceden
Frases. Las impulsa un ritmo:
Claro desfile de versos
Que sin romper el negror
De la noche a mí me alumbran.
Se funden cadencia y luz:
Palabra hacia poesía,
Que se cumple acaso en ti,
En tu instante de poeta,
Mi lector.

(*AN*, 1595)

Above the nocturnal silence,
phrases rise up and follow
one another. A rhythm impels them:
A bright parade of verses which,
without breaking the darkness
of the night, illumine me.
Cadence and light become fused:
The word [moves] toward poetry
which may be fulfilled in you,
in your moment as a poet,
my reader.

The initial two sentences (six lines) of the poem are quite similar in content to "Candelabrum." The poet speaks of darkness mitigated by the light of poetic creation. That inner process alone, however, is not the primary theme of the poem. As indicated by the title, Guillén here addresses the reader, his anonymous "collaborator" in the aesthetic process. In order for its destiny to be fulfilled, the poem must reach the interested reader, at which point it becomes communication and provides illumination for someone other than the solitary poet. The final dedication of *Homage*, "to the friend of the future" (*AN*, 1677), may well refer to this collaborator who will recreate the voice of the poet in future time.

Homage is a multifacted work in which Guillén reaffirms the most elemental values of his earlier poetry, and thus a most important collection for understanding the cycle of Guillén's evolution. Many themes and attitudes from *Cántico* reappear vividly in *Homage* after the hiatus of *Clamor*. The two themes discussed in this chapter are salient aspects of *Homage* in which Guillén utters in new ways his fundamental creed of existential optimism and joy. Despite advancing age, the same faith in a pervasive goodness in the world occupies a central position in *And Other Poems*, Guillén's last major collection published to date.

III *Age and Reminiscence in* And Other Poems

As indicated by the title, *Y otros poemas* [And Other Poems] is a collection in which Guillén continues to give voice to the salient themes of his previous collections. The title is also indicative of the fact that Guillén did not originally intend for his *Other Poems* to be an integral component of the compact unity that is *Our Air*. This initial decision was later changed, however, since the poet includes

And Other Poems in the projected definitive edition of his collected poetry (see bibliography).[4]

The principal topics of Guillén's *Other Poems* have on the whole been seen before, and most have been studied in the previous chapters. The affirmation of reality and love, the acceptance of finitude and death, the sense of outrage with the specter of the Franco dictatorship (Franco was still alive when the book was published in 1973), are familiar and moving themes from *Cántico, Clamor*, and *Homage*. An area of thought that receives special attention in *And Other Poems* is old age, not a new theme in Guillén's work, but one which becomes more personal in *And Other Poems*.[5] Guillén's decades-long trajectory of increased personal visibility in his work is especially apparent in his *Other Poems*, a collection in which it is often more appropriate to conceive of the author as "Guillén," than as a somewhat detached "poet" or "speaker." Since old age is the principal theme that distinguishes *And Other Poems* from other collections, this topic is the subject of the following brief discussion.

It is not surprising that old age should be a predominant theme in a collection that the author began to compose after passing the age of seventy.[6] Significantly, the treatment of aging in *And Other Poems* reflects the point of view of the poet himself throughout the collection. In the earlier works, aging is viewed primarily in secondary association with the concepts of time and finitude, the dominant ideas in poems treating mortality. Guillén typically maintains a certain aesthetic distance from his topic in those poems, so time and death can be analyzed philosophically or intellectually in a more or less objective manner. While thoroughly aware of his role as an artist in *And Other Poems*, he allows himself the liberty of a much more personal tone in this work. His attitude is seen clearly in the first poem from a series appropriately entitled "De Senectute" [On Old Age]:

> Sale el sol otra vez para el anciano.
> ¿Cuántas veces aún? Inútil cómputo
> De condenado a muerte. La luz sea
> Sin predicción precisa de adivino:
> Vital incertidumbre. Sale el sol.
>
> (*YOP*, 67)

> The sun rises another time for the old man.
> How many more times? A useless calculation
> by the man condemned to die. Let the light be,

without the precise prediction of a prophet:
Vital uncertainty. The sun rises.

In this short poem, thoughts of death are added to Guillén's predilection for the use of light as a poetic image. Light, always a symbol of life and spirit in Guillén's work, here continues to be an inspiration to the aging poet. In this context, it is worth remembering the initial lines from "Beyond," the first poem of *Cántico:* "Light! It floods my being with wonder" (*AN*, 26). The unabashed joy of the earlier poem is now tempered by the vision of age. Notably, however, Guillén chooses to conclude the poem with a repetititon of the image of life, not death. The attitude is one of humility and gratitude, mixed with awe.

The idea of passing time becomes very personal in *And Other Poems*. In "Anochecer" [Nightfall], a poem written in the coastal community of La Jolla, California, Guillén contemplates a palm tree with the sky and sea as background, at sunset:[7]

Se yergue una palmera,
Eje central de nuestra perspectiva
Con el cielo por fondo,
Materia inmaterial que se trasforma
Sin cesar en matices no gritados,
Rosa, gris, violeta de un instante
Como yo, como todo—fugitivo.

(*YOP*, 377)

A palm tree stands erect,
the center of our view
with the sky as background,
that immaterial substance that becomes increasingly
transformed into understated hues,
rose, gray, violet, [all] for an instant
—like myself, like all else—fleeting.

Thoughts of death and the fugitive nature of time come naturally to the aged poet as he compares himself and his immediate surroundings to the eternity of the sky and the sunset. The imagery of nightfall-darkness-death is balanced somewhat by the figure of the palm tree in the center of the scene. On one level of meaning, the palm might be identified with the poet since both are living entities and therefore have temporal limits. Also, however, the palm is a symbol of victory and wisdom, attributes that can be associated with old age.[8] So while the poet here places emphasis on time and on literal and figurative nightfall, the poem is not without an affirmative element as well.

In another, untitled poem, Guillén comments on the "victory" that old age represents:

> Yo he nacido en el siglo XIX,
> Y aquí estoy, jugador afortunado
> Por entre los innúmeros azares
> Hostiles, peligrosos en fronteras
> De riesgos sin cesar amenazantes.
> Vejez es ya victoria. Yo sonrío
> Con gratitud a la Fortuna cómplice.
>
> (*YOP*, 495)

> I was born in the nineteenth century,
> and here I am, a fortunate gambler
> among the countless hostile,
> dangerous hazards on the borders
> of unceasingly threatening risks.
> Old age [itself] is a victory. I smile
> with thanks at my accomplice, Fortune.

This very direct poem gains in significance when one considers the age of the poet and the indication of fulfillment in the course of a long life. The reaffirmation of the youthful happiness that springs from every page of *Cántico* underscores the enduring value of Guillén's fundamental optimism. Poems such as this in *And Other Poems* constitute a reiteration of the affirmative stance of the poet despite the negativity that he confronts—and overcomes—in *Clamor*. In *And Other Poems,* therefore, Guillén continues the tendency of *Homage* to restate the optimistic themes of fulfillment, reinforced by the additional life experience that accompanies age.

That the poet can continue to reaffirm his basic optimism in old age is a tribute to the indomitable qualities of human spirit expressed so admirably in his art. The fact that negative elements occasionally intrude on this last collection—as they intrude on all Guillén's works—is indicative of the poet's philosophy that misfortune and despair should not be sublimated in the ivory tower of art, but rather confronted squarely and thus transcended. So it is that Guillén can steadfastly affirm, after a half-century of resounding optimism before the reality of the world:

Luces eléctricas abajo.
Arriba emerge banda roja.
Ya cielo con suelo contrajo
Matrimonio de nube a hoja.
Río, calles, torres, ciudad
Aguardan al sol: la verdad.

(*YOP*, 51)

Electric lights below.
Above, a red border emerges.
Now heaven and earth have arranged
the marriage of cloud and leaf.
The river, streets, towers and city
await the sun: the truth.

CHAPTER 5

Conclusion

DIVERSITY within unity is perhaps the common denominator of Jorge Guillén's vast poetic output. The massive volume *Our Air* is an organic unity which reflects a totality of intuition, vision, and intellect. And yet, each individual component of the totality is itself an independent entity—there are constant factors in Guillén's affirmation and reaffirmation of his basic values, but the poet avoids the pitfall of monotonous repetition by his evolution toward new themes and expression. Therefore, the present study has focused on the distinctive features of each collection.

To insist obstinately on the timeless, "pure" qualities of Guillén's work would be to ignore the full breadth of his poetic imagination and the originality of each major work. The unifying element in this poetry is the world view—the *Weltanschauung*—of a poet deeply committed to the celebration of a life made meaningful by love, art, and harmony with nature. So it is that Guillén in his poetic works can momentarily turn away from the optimism of *Cántico* and confront negation directly *(Clamor)*, then return to his fundamental poetic stance of saying "yes" to his—and our—world *(Homage, And Other Poems)*.

Optimism and joy are the most basic and enduring characteristics of Guillén's poetic vision, even when *Clamor* is taken into consideration with the other works. It is somewhat of a critical commonplace to maintain that *Clamor* represents, in Guillén's poetic evolution, the negative side of life that does not enter into the world of *Cántico*. Under examination, however, this generalization loses credence. The second volume of *Clamor, We Will End at the Sea*, deals with death and dying, but in an ultimately affirmative manner inasmuch as the speaker, by accepting his human finitude, gains in nobility and even in vitality, living each day to the fullest. Furthermore, it would be incorrect to conceive of this collection as being "committed" poetry—another generalization applied to *Clamor*—since the literary treatment of death is as old as literature and philosophy, and is certainly not limited to the poetry of commitment as the genre has developed in the twentieth century. The third volume of *Clamor*, on the other hand, *To Rise to the Occasion*, thematically has more in common with *Cántico* and *Homage* than with the first two volumes of *Clamor*. *Sea of Confusion* is, of course, a "committed" work and has given the "social" label to *Clamor* as a whole. But *Sea of Confusion* contains 168 printed pages of poetry, and Guillén's total production to date far exceeds two thousand pages. These figures indicate that the socially committed aspect of Guillén's work is proportionally quite limited, and that his posture of affirmation is the dominant feature of his total poetic production. Even the dedication of *Clamor*—"to possible hope"—seems to underscore the poet's true feelings.

Guillén's essential unity of vision, combined with a delicate and superbly controlled poetic style, endow the poet with a rare permanence that is increasingly appreciated by readers of his work. Ironically, the poet who was once labeled as being too "cold" and "intellectual" to be of much interest is today seen to have created works of genuinely timeless value, while many works of his contemporaries now appear as relics of a bygone period in aesthetic experimentation. Esteem for Jorge Guillén's litany to life's best and most enduring aspirations and realizations will surely increase, as readers continue to appreciate how unfettered by time, place, and circumstance his poetry really is. By his "rise to the occasion" as a universal poet, he has created an art that transcends national and temporal limitations.

Another guarantee of the enduring worth and acceptance of Guillén's work is his undaunted, unfailing "yes" to the great world around us. The poet's delight with the gifts of life, love, and the grandeur of the enveloping macrocosm make his hymnal of affirmation seem forever fresh and newly charged with vitality. With Jorge Guillén's admirable optimism in mind, this study can be brought to a close with a poem that is profound and yet charmingly concise in all that is summarized in it—one which an aging poet might choose to sum up a life's work and a world view:

> En un bar que se llama "Cosmos"
> Don Jorge toma su café,

Pone el pensamiento en los astros
Y ya es feliz con lo que ve.

(*YOP*, 490)

In a bar named "Cosmos,"
Don Jorge has his coffee,
thinks of the stars,
and is happy with what he sees.

Notes and References

Chapter One

1. For a general consideration of these two movements, see Guillermo Díaz-Plaja, *Modernismo frente a noventa y ocho* (Madrid, 1951).

2. C. B. Morris, in *A Generation of Spanish Poets, 1920–1936* (Cambridge, 1969), p. 120, points out succinctly that Guillén's *interest* in Valéry has often been interpreted erroneously as influence. Thorough considerations of the issue are found in Antonio Blanch, *La poesía pura española: Conexiones con la cultura francesa* (Madrid, 1976), pp. 284–303; Biruté Ciplijauskaité, *Deber de plenitud: La poesía de Jorge Guillén* (Mexico City, 1973), pp. 87–111; and Concha Zardoya, *Poesía española del 98 y del 27* Madrid, 1968), pp. 207–54.

3. The most complete study of Ultraism-Creationism in Spain is Gloria Videla, *El ultraísmo: Estudios sobre movimientos de vanguardia* (Madrid, 1963). For a concise summary of the movement, see John Crispin, *Pedro Salinas* (New York, 1974), pp. 17–20. For an overall study, see Guillermo de Torre, *Historia de las literaturas de vanguardia,* 3 vols. (Madrid, 1974).

4. In *Language and Poetry: Some Poets of Spain* (Cambridge, Massachusetts, 1961), p. 204. Other concise summaries of the Spanish reaction to surrealism are found in Ciplijauskaité, pp. 24–25, and Carl W. Cobb, *Contemporary Spanish Poetry (1898–1963)* (Boston, 1976), pp. 68–70.

5. Antonio Oliver, "Dos horas con Jorge Guillén en el Museo del Prado," *Indice,* November 15, 1951, pp. 1–2.

6. "Carta a Fernando Vela," *Revista de Occidente* 14 (1926): 234.

7. *Language and Poetry,* p. 205. The ideal of pure poetry united the poets to the extent that one leading critic of the group, Andrew P. Debicki, feels that a shared vision of the function of poetry was what the different authors had most in common. See his *Estudios sobre poesía española contemporánea* (Madrid, 1968), pp. 17–39. On the aesthetics of the Generation, see also Ciplijauskaité, *El poeta y la poesía* (Madrid, 1966), pp. 273–382.

8. Morris, p. 119.

9. Ibid., pp. 97–100.

10. Ciplijauskaité, *Deber de plenitud,* p. 16.

11. Luis Cernuda, *Estudios sobre poesía española contemporánea* (Madrid, 1957), p. 99. Morris, pp. 134–137, argues convincingly that Cernuda may have been critical of Guillén because of a literary debt that he did not wish to acknowledge, despite the vastly different outlooks in the authors' works.

12. Quoted in Guillén's prolog to Lorca's *Obras completas,* ed. Arturo del Hoyo, 11th ed. (Madrid, 1966), p. lvii. Lorca's *Romancero gitano* and

the first edition of *Cántico* were both published in 1928 by Revista de Occidente.

13. On the permanent value of Guillén's poetry as compared to some of the more extreme expressions of contemporary literature, see Ivar Ivask, "Poesía integral en una era de desintegración," in *Jorge Guillén,* ed. Ciplijauskaité (Madrid, 1975), pp. 31–46.

14. *Poetas españoles contemporáneos,* 3d ed. (Madrid, 1965), p. 160.

15. Crispin, p. 21; Morris, p. 23.

16. For the first message, see Jiménez, *Selección de cartas (1899–1958)* (Barcelona, 1973), p. 99; the second is quoted in Joaquín Caro Romero, *Jorge Guillén* (Madrid, 1974), p. 57. For Jiménez's later judgments on the Generation of 1927, see his "Crisis del espíritu en la poesía española contemporánea," *Nosotros* 48 (1940): 165–82; see also *Españoles de tres mundos* (Buenos Aires, 1942), pp. 105–6. The most complete account of the exchange between Guillén and Jiménez appears in *Indice* (edición para el extranjero), March 30, 1954, pp. 1 ff. See also Morris, pp. 10–11.

17. Exhaustively detailed in Ian Gibson, *The Death of Lorca* (Chicago, 1973).

18. A personal memory may be of some relevance. During a visit to Spain in 1967, I found the *Thoughts* of Mao Tse Tung on sale openly in Madrid bookstores. But Guillén's *Maremágnum* [Sea of Confusion], with its strong poem about an apocryphal military dictator, "Potencia de Pérez" ("The Power of Pérez"), was not to be found.

19. Personal letter, November 18, 1973.

20. Claude Couffon, *Dos encuentros con Jorge Guillén* (Paris, n.d. [1963]), p. 14.

21. Guillén's years at Wellesley are described by Justina Ruiz de Conde, *El cántico americano de Jorge Guillén* (Madrid, 1973), pp. 252–75.

22. Personal letter, June 20, 1979.

23. Personal letter, October 17, 1972.

Chapter Two

1. Guillén makes this statement in the introduction to *Cántico: A Selection,* ed. Norman Thomas di Giovanni (Boston, 1965), p. 4.

2. The 1928 edition of *Cántico* has been republished (Paris, 1962), but not as a facsimile nor as a critical edition of the first.

3. "Jorge Guillén: A Poet of This Time," *Atlantic Monthly,* January, 1961, p. 128.

4. Guillén was thirty-five years old when *Cántico* was first published. In contrast, García Lorca published his first collection at the age of twenty-three (1921), and Pedro Salinas published three poems before age twenty (1911).

5. *Al aire de tu vuelo* [In the Wake of Your Wings], *Las horas situadas* [The Designated Hours], *El pájaro en la mano* [The Bird in the Hand], *Aquí mismo* [Here and Now], *Pleno ser* [Fullness of Being].

6. An example of Guillén's attention to detail is the sonnet, "Amanece, amanezco" [The Day Dawns, I Awaken], the manuscript of which runs to forty-four pages. Reprinted in facsimile in Manuel Alvar, *Visión en claridad: Estudios sobre "Cántico"* (Madrid, 1976), pp. 193–236.

7. Richard Chandler and Kessel Schwartz, *A New History of Spanish Literature* (Baton Rouge, 1961), p. 385.

8. Couffon, p. 11. Guillén refers to the unfortunately ambiguous term "dehumanization" of art, coined by the Spanish philosopher Ortega y Gasset to characterize the tendency of most modern artists to move away from nineteenth-century realism. Guillén here echoes an error of many contemporaries: Ortega did not propose "dehumanization" as an aesthetic formula. He merely described a trend.

9. Juan Chabás goes so far as to describe *Cántico* as "una poesía *egoísta*, de egoísmo absoluto" ("an *egotistical* poetry, of absolute egotism"), *Literatura española contemporánea, 1898–1950* (Havana, 1952), p. 518.

10. *Historia de la literatura española,* 7th ed. (Barcelona, 1964), 3:655.

11. *Aire nuestro* (Milan, 1968), p. 316. Except where noted, all references are to this edition, and are indicated in the text with the abbreviation *AN*.

12. See John A. Mourant, "*Scientia Media* and Molinism," in *The Encyclopedia of Philosophy,* ed. Paul Edwards (New York, 1967), 7:338.

13. *El argumento de la obra* (Barcelona, 1969), p. 51.

14. Ibid.

15. The poem was first published in *Revista de Occidente* 48 (1935):1–10.

16. In his thorough study, Andrew P. Debicki, *La poesía de Jorge Guillén* (Madrid, 1973), comments in detail on Guillén's view of his poetic role. See pp. 57–62 for Debicki's discussion of "Beyond," which he interprets as being in great part a declaration of Guillén's own aesthetics. For other interpretations of the poem, see Joaquín González Muela, *La realidad y Jorge Guillén* (Madrid, 1962), pp. 81–90, and Joaquín Casalduero, *"Cántico" de Jorge Guillén y "Aire nuestro"* (Madrid, 1974), pp. 94–99.

17. *Obras completas,* 11th ed. (Madrid, 1964), p. 477. Since "Beyond" is the first poem of *Cántico,* it is also interesting to note the following lines from the initial poem of Pedro Salinas' first published collection, *Presagios* [Presages, 1924]: "Suelo. Nada más. / Suelo. Nada menos. / Y que te baste con eso" ("Earth. Nothing more. Earth. Nothing less. And may that suffice you.") *Poesías completas,* ed. Soledad Salinas de Marichal (Barcelona, 1971), p. 53.

18. Nietzsche's influence in Spain has been documented and chronicled in Gonzalo Sobjejano's extensive study, *Nietzsche en España* (Madrid, 1967). For Salinas's views, see especially the series of poems entitled "Todo

más claro" [All Things Made Clearer], from the collection of the same title (in Salinas's *Poesías completas*, pp. 597–607).

19. Northrup Frye observes a similar distinction between "centrifugal" (directed outward) and "centripetal" (directed inward) poetry. See *The Anatomy of Criticism* (Princeton, 1957), p. 73.

20. John B. Noss, *Man's Religions*, 3d ed. (New York, 1963), pp. 330–31.

21. Among Guillén's contemporaries, Juan Ramón Jiménez probably exploits the image of the tree more than any other author. For a thorough consideration of this type of symbolism, see Rupert C. Allen, "Juan Ramón and the World Tree: A Symbological Analysis of Mysticism in the Poetry of Juan Ramón Jiménez, " *Revista Hispánica Moderna* 35 (1969): 306–22.

22. Readers of Spanish are aware that the expression "agua abajo" has the idiomatic meaning "downstream" in addition to my more literal translation "with water below." I have chosen the latter translation as it seems more suitable to the context of the poem.

23. Willis Barnstone, "The Greeks, San Juan, and Jorge Guillén," in *Luminous Reality: The Poetry of Jorge Guillén*, ed. Ivar Ivask and Juan Marichal (Norman, 1969), p. 29; Casalduero, p. 15; Martha LaFollette Miller, "Love in the Poetry of Jorge Guillén" (Ph.D. diss., Washington University, 1972), pp. 14–15. On the religiosity of Guillén's erotic poetry, see Carolyn Pinet, "The Sacramental View of Poetry and the Religion of Love in Jorge Guillén's *Cántico*," *Hispania* 62 (1979): 47–55.

24. Debicki, *Guillén*, p. 103.

25. Readers wishing to examine in a variety of contexts Guillén's use of "desnudar" ("to denude"), "desnudez," and "desnudo," can refer to *Aire nuestro*, pp. 46, 48, 103, 113, 165, 183, 186, 220, 249, 312, 321, 331, 403, 494. This list is not exhaustive, but is broadly representative of the poet's usage.

26. The notion of the overpowering quality of sexual climax ("let the imminence conclude") is stated quite similarly in "A Springtime Salvation": "¿Lo infinito? No. Cesa / La angustia insostenible" ("The infinite? No. The / unbearable anxiety ceases"), *AN*, 109.

27. See Miller, "Transcendence Through Love in Jorge Guillén's *Cántico:* The Conciliation of Inner and Outer Reality," *Modern Language Notes* 92 (1977): 312–25.

28. A discussion of the religious overtones of this poem would seem to lie beyond the theme of time under consideration. Guillén's religious attitudes will be examined briefly with the consideration of death in *Cántico*. It is worth noting, however, that Guillén did not consciously intend for the poem to be of religious meaning or significance. Personal letter, April 8, 1972.

29. See, e.g., C. G. Jung, *Psychology and Alchemy*, in *The Collected Works of C. G. Jung*, trans. R. F. C. Hull, 2d ed. (Princeton, 1968), 12:117–19, 174–75.

30. This poem apparently made a deep impression on Federico García Lorca. In his powerful work on modern alienation and rootlessness, *Poeta en Nueva York* [Poet in New York], Lorca in one poem, "Tu infancia en Menton" [Your Childhood in Menton], quotes Guillén's final line as an epigraph, then uses it three times in his own poem as an ironic contrast to adult life in the present. See *Obras completas,* pp. 475–76.

31. Winter is not categorically seen in a negative light in *Cántico*. Cf. "Autumn Branch" and "With or Without Snow," discussed above, and "Luminous Night," below.

32. This is the only use in *Cántico* of the phrase "aire nuestro" ("our air"), the title Guillén later chose for his collected poems. It is a reminder of the unity in Guillén's poetry that, despite much evolution over the years, the title for the 1968 collected poems comes from a poem published in 1924, four years before the first edition of *Cántico*.

33. See "Descanso en jardín" [Rest in a Garden, *AN*, 75], "Vida urbana" [Urban Life, *AN*, 94], "Más vida" [More Life, *AN*, 392]. Additionally, there is one four line poem, "Camposanto" [Churchyard, *AN*, 266], in which death is seen as an escape from war. It is an extremely rare pessimistic poem that first appeared in the 1945 edition of *Cántico,* which would indicate that the poem was written during the Spanish Civil War or World War II.

34. Couffon, p. 34.

35. These statements and others referred to below are extracted from various conversations I have been fortunate to have had with Professor Guillén since July, 1970. While I hope to avoid the pitfall of intentional fallacy when discussing specific poems, it seems to me that, as the topic is one which borders on philosophy in spirit if not in discipline, it is relevant to examine the intellectual foundation of the poems under consideration. See my "Death in *Cántico:* Jorge Guillén and Martin Heidegger," *Romance Notes* (1982), in press.

36. Martin Heidegger, *Being and Time,* trans. John Macquarrie and Edward Robinson (New York, 1962), pp. 293–311. Heidegger is often best approached through secondary sources. For a concise and readable presentation of his thought regarding death, see Jacques Choron, *Death and Western Thought* (New York, 1963), pp. 230–40. Historically, it is interesting to note that Heidegger's first edition of *Sein und Zeit* appeared in 1927, one year before the first edition of *Cántico*.

37. Heidegger, p. 297; Choron, p. 234.

38. Heidegger, pp. 299–304; Choron, p. 235. In *Cántico: A Selection,* p. 6, Guillén states that the image of the wall as a boundary was inspired by a cemetery wall in his birthplace, Valladolid. José Luis Cano, "La muerte en la poesía de Jorge Guillén," *Insula,* July–August, 1977, p. 17, uses the poem to illustrate the idea that optimism is given priority over death in Guillén's work. Casalduero, pp. 81–86, reads the sonnet as a combination of abstract realization of natural law and knowledge of personal mortality.

Debicki, *Guillén*, pp. 29–31, includes the poem in exposition of his thesis that *Cántico* is a union of concrete experiences and universal truths. Julian Palley, in the notes to his translation, *Affirmation: A Bilingual Anthology, 1919–1966* (Norman, 1968), pp. 192–94, comments on the idea of acceptance; the same commentary is published in *The Poem Itself*, ed. Stanley Burnshaw (New York, 1960): pp. 214–16.

39. See Guillén, *Cántico (1936)*, ed. José Manuel Blecua (Barcelona, 1970), p. 39. In this model critical edition, Blecua traces the changes in all the poems which comprise the 1936 edition of *Cántico*, from their first appearance (often in journals) to their final form in the 1968 *Aire nuestro*.

40. Casalduero examines the theme of unity in *Cántico*, which he frequently relates to the circle; see especially pp. 54–61, 76–79, 315. Eugenio Frutos, in Ivask and Marichal, pp. 75–81, comments on the idea of perfection and its antagonizing forces, which he similarly relates to the circle. Robert J. Havard, "The Early *décimas* of Jorge Guillén," *Bulletin of Hispanic Studies* 48 (1971): 111–27, indicates that circular symbolism is a theme which Guillén uses from his earliest work, and also comments on the archetypal significance of the circle. Georges Poulet, *The Metamorphoses of the Circle*, trans. Elliott Coleman and Carley Dawson (Baltimore, 1966), pp. 347–50, compares Guillén's use of circular imagery with that of other Occidental authors from the past; Poulet concentrates on the primacy of the outside world in *Cántico*, which manifests itself to the individual in circular patterns and rhythms.

41. For a detailed consideration of the archetypal foundations of Guillén's geometrical symbolism, see my "Mandala: The Culmination of *Cántico*," *Hispanófila* 24 (1980): 57–69.

42. See Mircea Eliade, *Yoga: Immortality and Freedom*, trans. Willard R. Trask (New York, 1958), p. 225. For general background, see Giuseppe Tucci, *The Theory and Practice of the Mandala*, trans. Alan Houghton Brodrick (London, 1961).

43. Jung, *Psychology and Religion: West and East*, in *The Collected Works of C. G. Jung*, trans. R. F. C. Hull, 2d ed. (New York, 1963), 11:82.

44. Guillén, *Cántico (1936)*, pp. 17–18.

45. Personal letter, April 8, 1972.

46. Couffon, p. 29.

47. On poetic creation, see "Hacia el poema" [Toward the Poem, *AN*, 273]; on the recreation of reality in poetry, see "Los nombres" [The Names, *AN*, 36], and especially "Bosque y bosque" [The Forest and the Forest, *AN*, 331]; on the reality of poetry, see "Tu realidad" [Your Reality, *AN*, 406]. For a brief study of the archetypal elements involved in poetic intuition and recreation in Guillén's poetry, see my "La estética y la psique: 'Bosque y bosque' de Jorge Guillén," *Explicación de Textos Literarios* 2 (1973): 75–79.

48. This sentence might alternately be translated, "the afternoon is removed from the man and his possible company [companion]," in which

case "company" would refer to the possible reader, who is described and then addressed later in the poem. The translation given in the text is in keeping with the context of the initial strophes, in which Guillén emphasizes the interaction of the poet and the reality of the world.

49. There is a similar attitude in the Platonic notion of the romantic poet Bécquer, mentioned above, for whom a poem is an approximate image of the ideal of Poetry, as in the first poem of the *Rimas* [Poems], in *Obras completas*, p. 435.

50. For other interpretations of "Utmost Life," see Debicki, *Guillén*, pp. 67–71; González Muela, pp. 136–43; and Pinet (see n. 23). On Guillén's poetics, see Ciplijauskaité, *Deber de plenitud*, pp. 37–54.

51. For more detailed information on the transition from *Cántico* to *Clamor*, see José Ortega, "Conjunción y oposición en J. Guillén: De *Cántico* a *Clamor*," *Cuadernos Hispanoamericanos* 318 (1976): 542–49, and Robert J. Weber, "De *Cántico* a *Clamor*," *Revista Hispánica Moderna* 29 (1963): 109–19. For the poet's comments, see Couffon, p. 24.

52. Personal letter, February 23, 1976.

Chapter Three

1. For a somewhat extreme view of Guillén's evolution toward *Clamor*, see José María Castellet, *Veinte años de poesía española (1939–1959)*, 3d ed. (Barcelona, 1962), pp. 90–92. More balanced perspectives are found in Debicki, *Guillén*, pp. 228–55, Palley, "Jorge Guillén and the Poetry of Commitment," *Hispania* 45 (1962): 689–91, and Zardoya, "*Clamor I:* Stylistic Peculiarities," in Ivask and Marichal, pp. 145–78. In general, it should be noted that *Clamor* has received relatively little attention from critics in comparison with Guillén's other works.

2. For another consideration of this poem, see Debicki, *Guillén*, pp. 162–63, 308–9.

3. Couffon, p. 18.

4. Limitations of space preclude the discussion of poems that essentially reinforce the point of view expressed in *Cántico*. Two lengthy poems should be noted, however: "Una exposición" [An Exposition, *AN*, 768–73], on the subject of agnosticism, and "Soy mortal" [I Am Mortal, *AN*, 868–71], on the acceptance of death.

5. Couffon, p. 27. The principal studies of *To Rise to the Occasion* are Ciplijauskaité, "*Clamor* a la altura de las circunstancias," *Revista Hispánica Moderna* 29 (1963): 290–97; see also Debicki, *Estudios sobre poesía española contemporánea*, pp. 135–49, and *Guillén*, pp. 32–42. Although these studies differ somewhat in focus, they are in essential agreement with one another and with the present analysis. *To Rise to the Occasion* is not the type of collection that lends itself to widely divergent interpretations, and there is no real critical disagreement regarding the work.

Chapter Four

1. For a concise interpretation of *Homage* as a synthesis of *Cántico* and *Clamor*, see Ivar Ivask, "On First Looking Into Guillén's *Homenaje*," in Ivask and Marichal, pp. 124–30. See also Ignacio Prat, *"Aire nuestro" de Jorge Guillén* (Barcelona, 1974), p. 192, and Oreste Macrí, *La obra poética de Jorge Guillén* (Barcelona, 1976), p. 411. Emilia de Zuleta, "La poesía de Jorge Guillén," in *Cinco poetas españoles* (Madrid, 1971), pp. 108–67, concentrates on the basic themes of *Cántico* in Guillén's later work, but devotes most of her attention to *Clamor*, and mentions *Homage* only in passing. See also my "The Erotic Poetry of Jorge Guillén's *Homenaje*," *Hispania* 65 (1982): in press.

2. See, e.g., Jung, *Aion: Researches Into the Phenomenology of the Self*, in *The Collected Works of C. G. Jung*, trans. R. F. C. Hull (New York, 1959), vol. 9. pt. 2: 11–22.

3. The principal metapoetic interpretations of *Homage* are Ciplijauskaité, "Una gloria ya madura bajo mi firme decisión," in Ivask and Marichal, pp. 34–48, and Debicki, *Guillén*, pp. 42, 45, 47, 55, 89, 95, 278–80, 282.

4. Personal interview, March, 1975; personal letter, February 23, 1976.

5. See Ivask, " 'Grand âge, nous ici': Some Remarks on the Theme of Old Age in Jorge Guillén's Poetry," in *Homenaje a Jorge Guillén*, ed. Justina Ruiz de Conde, et al. (Madrid, 1978), pp. 277–83.

6. *Y otros poemas* (Buenos Aires, 1973), p. 8; all references are to this edition, henceforth abbreviated *YOP* in the text.

7. Personal interview, March, 1972.

8. On the symbolism of the palm, see Jung, *Psychology and Religion*, p. 388; also Erich Neumann, *The Great Mother: An Analysis of the Archetype*, trans. Ralph Manheim, 2d ed. (New York, 1963), pp. 241–45.

Selected Bibliography

The list of primary sources includes all poetic works published as complete collections. The prose works included are those mentioned in the notes. The bibliography on Guillén's poetry is extensive, and the list of secondary sources is not exhaustive. In addition to works referred to in the notes, I have attempted to include other salient studies that contain valuable contributions to the critical dialogue concerning Guillén's poetry. The most complete bibliography on Guillén appears in Oreste Macrí's study, while the most useful annotated bibliography is found in Andrew P. Debicki's volume on the poet.

With the exception of a final section of miscellaneous secondary sources which clearly do not deal directly with Guillén's work, I have not attempted to distinguish between critical studies of the poet himself and studies of contemporary poetry which contain material on Guillén, as such a division tends to become unavoidably arbitrary.

PRIMARY SOURCES

1. Original poetic works in Spanish (listed chronologically)

Cántico. Madrid: Revista de Occidente, 1928. The first edition of *Cántico*. 75 poems, 171 pages.

Cántico. Edited by Claude Couffon. Paris: Centre de Recherches de l'Institut d'Etudes Hispaniques, 1962. A reprint of the 1928 edition. 101 pages.

Cántico. 2d ed. Madrid: Cruz y Raya, 1936. The second edition of *Cántico*. 125 poems, 306 pages.

Cántico (1936). Edited by José Manuel Blecua. Barcelona: Labor, 1970. An excellent critical edition of the 1936 *Cántico*, with a valuable introductory study. 243 pages.

Cántico: Fe de vida. 3d ed. Mexico City: Litoral, 1945. The third edition of *Cántico*. 270 poems, 412 pages.

Cántico: Fe de vida. 1st complete ed. Buenos Aires: Sudamericana, 1950. The fourth edition of *Cántico*, the first of the work in its complete form. 334 poems, 540 pages. Reprinted in 1962 and 1973 as 2d and 3d complete eds.

Clamor: Tiempo de historia. Vol 1. *Maremágnum*. Buenos Aires: Sudamericana, 1957. The first volume of *Clamor*. 204 pages.

Clamor: Tiempo de historia. Vol. 2. *. . . Que van a dar en la mar*. Buenos Aires: Sudamericana, 1960. The second volume of *Clamor*. 202 pages.

Clamor: Tiempo de historia. Vol. 3. *A la altura de las circunstancias*. Buenos Aires: Sudamericana, 1963. The final volume of *Clamor*. 178 pages.

Homenaje: Reunión de vidas. Milan: All'Insegna del Pesce d'Oro, 1967. 630 pages.

Aire nuestro: Cántico, Clamor, Homenaje. Milan: All'Insegna del Pesce d'Oro, 1968. The publication in one volume of Guillén's first three major collections. 1698 pages.

Y otros poemas. Buenos Aires: Muchnik, 1973. 539 pages.

Final. In preparation. Guillén's last collection.

Aire nuestro: Cántico, Clamor, Homenaje, Y otros poemas, Final. Barcelona: Barral, in press. The planned definitive edition of Guillén's complete poetry.

2. English translations of poetic works

Affirmation: A Bilingual Anthology, 1919–1966. Translated by Julian Palley. Introduction by Jorge Guillén. Norman: University of Oklahoma Press, 1968. A largely accurate and readable translation. The introductory essay by Guillén appears in Spanish in *El argumento de la obra* (see below). 204 pages.

Cántico: A Selection. Edited by Norman Thomas di Giovanni. Introduction by Jorge Guillén. Boston: Little, Brown, 1965. Translations by a number of collaborators. Very uneven in accuracy and quality. 291 pages.

Guillén on Guillén. Translated by Reginald Gibbons and Anthony L. Geist. Princeton: Princeton University Press, 1979. Useful translations and informal comments by the poet. 220 pages.

3. Selected prose works, including interviews

"Carta a Fernando Vela." *Revista de Occidente* 14 (1926): 234. Guillén's concise and often-quoted definition of pure poetry.

COUFFON, CLAUDE. *Dos encuentros con Jorge Guillén*. Paris: Centre de Recherches de l'Institut d'Etudes Hispaniques, n.d. (1963). Two penetrating interviews on topics related to the aesthetics of Guillén and his contemporaries. Especially useful are Guillén's remarks on the occasionally exaggerated concept of pure poetry, and on the relationship between *Cántico* and *Clamor*. 31 pages.

El argumento de la obra. Barcelona: Sinera, 1969. Three essays on poetry, including an extremely useful commentary on *Cántico*. 109 pages.

Federico en persona. Buenos Aires: Emecé, 1959. An interpretive and appreciative essay on García Lorca; includes correspondence. 143 pages.

FUENTE LAFUENTE, ISMAEL. "Jorge Guillén, 84 años de poesía." *El País Semanal*, January 23, 1977, pp. 4–5. A brief interview on primarily personal topics.

"J. Guillén replica a Juan Ramón J." *Indice* (edición para el extranjero), March 30, 1954, pp. 1ff. A thorough summary of the disagreement between Guillén and Jiménez; includes Guillén's own comments.

Language and Poetry: Some Poets of Spain. Cambridge: Harvard University Press, 1961. The public lectures that Guillén delivered during his visiting professorship at Harvard. Contains an essay on the Generation of 1927. 293 pages.

Lenguaje y poesía: Algunos casos españoles. Madrid: Revista de Occidente, 1962. The Spanish version of *Language and Poetry*. 269 pages.

OLIVER, ANTONIO. "Dos horas con Jorge Guillén en el Museo del Prado." *Indice*, November 15, 1951, pp. 1–2. A brief interview on Guillén's work and on the Generation of 1927; special reference to Antonio Machado's importance in modern poetry.

SECONDARY SOURCES

1. Jorge Guillén and contemporary Spanish poetry

ALLEN, RUPERT C. "Notes on Self-Transcendence East and West: Jorge Guillén and Haiku." *Dieciocho: Hispanic Enlightenment, Aesthetics and Literary Theory* 1 (1978): 160–81. A penetrating, profoundly thoughtful essay on the symbological relationship between Guillén's shorter poetry, particularly the décima form, and the Japanese haiku.

ALONSO, DAMASO. *Poetas españoles contemporáneos*. 3d ed. Madrid: Gredos, 1965. A standard work on themes and poets. Contains an essay on Guillén, and one on the Generation of 1927.

ALVAR, MANUEL. *Visión en claridad: Estudios sobre "Cántico."* Madrid: Gredos, 1976. Linguistic analysis; also contains an interesting and instructive facsimile.

BARNSTONE, WILLIS. "The Greeks, San Juan, and Jorge Guillén." In Ivask and Marichal, *Luminous Reality: The Poetry of Jorge Guillén* (see below). An excellent thematic study of Greek notions regarding external reality and body/mind duality, and how these concepts are transformed in Guillén's poetry.

BATES, MARGARET. "Guillén's 'Advenimiento.' " *Explicator* 26 (1967) Art. no. 3.

BLANCH, ANTONIO. *La poesía pura española: Conexiones con la cultura francesa*. Madrid: Gredos, 1976. Contains a section on Guillén and Paul Valéry.

BOBES NAVES, MARIA DEL CARMEN. *Gramática de "Cántico": Análisis semiológico*. Barcelona: Planeta, 1975. Linguistic analysis.

CANO, JOSE LUIS. "La muerte en la poesía de Jorge Guillén." *Insula*, July–August, 1977, p. 17. A very brief article on Guillén's lack of despair as he confronts the idea of death.

———. *La poesía de la generación del 27*. Madrid: Guadarrama, 1970. Somewhat casual observations and personal reminiscences.

CARO ROMERO, JOAQUIN. *Jorge Guillén*. Madrid: Epesa, 1974. A brief anthology and introductory study, with emphasis placed on Guillén's life and personality.

CASALDUERO, JOAQUIN. *"Cántico" de Jorge Guillén y "Aire nuestro."* Madrid: Gredos, 1974. Republication of an earlier study (Madrid: Victoriano Suárez, 1953) with some additional material. A thematic study and survey of *Cántico*. Contains versification tables.

CASTELLET, JOSE MARIA. *Veinte años de poesía española*. 3d ed. Barcelona: Seix Barral, 1962. An anthology with a lengthy critical introduction. Contains some commentary on Guillén's shift from *Cántico* to *Clamor*.

CERNUDA, LUIS. *Estudios sobre poesía española contemporánea*. Madrid: Guadarrama, 1957. Subjective essays on trends and poets.

CIPLIJAUSKAITE, BIRUTE. "*Clamor* a la altura de las circunstancias." *Revista Hispánica Moderna* 29 (1963): 290–97. A concise overview of *To Rise to the Occasion*.

———. *Deber de plenitud: La poesía de Jorge Guillén*. Mexico City: SepSetentas, 1973. A collection of insightful essays on Guillén's work, especially with regard to his aesthetics.

———. *El poeta y la poesía*. Madrid: Insula, 1966. Contains a valuable chapter on the aesthetics of the Generation of 1927.

———, ed. *Jorge Guillén*. Madrid: Taurus, 1975. A useful anthology of articles on various aspects and stages of Guillén's work; most reprinted.

———. "Una gloria ya madura bajo mi firme decisión." In Ivask and Marichal, *Luminous Reality: The Poetry of Jorge Guillén* (see below). A succinct overview of *Homage*.

COBB, CARL. *Contemporary Spanish Poetry (1898–1963)*. Boston: Twayne, 1976. A survey in English of the major trends and authors.

CRISPIN, JOHN. *Pedro Salinas*. New York: Twayne, 1974. A good study in English of the work of Guillén's closest friend. Contains valuable background information on the Generation of 1927.

DARMANGEAT, PIERRE. *Antonio Machado, Pedro Salinas, Jorge Guillén*. Translated by J. L. Guereña. Madrid: Insula, 1969. Concentrates on unity and continuity in Guillén's work.

DEBICKI, ANDREW P. *Estudios sobre poesía española contemporánea*. Madrid: Gredos, 1968. An insightful study of major themes favored by several contemporary poets. Contains a particularly useful chapter on the aesthetics of the Generation of 1927.

———. *La poesía de Jorge Guillén*. Madrid: Gredos, 1973. Arguably the most thorough study of Guillén's work; special emphasis on the poet's aesthetics.

DEHENNIN, ELSA. *Cántico de Jorge Guillén: Une poésie de la clarté*. Brussels: University Press of Brussels, 1969. A monograph on the author's theory that light is the primary theme in *Cántico*.

DIAZ-PLAJA, GUILLERMO. *Modernismo frente a noventa y ocho*. Madrid: Espasa-Calpe, 1951. A study of these two early twentieth-century movements.

DIEZ DE REVENGA, FRANCISCO JAVIER. *La métrica de los poetas del 27*. Murcia: University of Murcia, 1973. Approaches to the Generation of 1927 based on the metrics used by the poets.

FRUTOS, EUGENIO. "El existencialismo jubiloso de Jorge Guillén." In Ciplijauskaité, *Jorge Guillén* (see above). An essay on Guillén's optimistic vision of reality.

———. "The Circle and Its Rupture in the Poetry of Jorge Guillén." In Ivask and Marichal, *Luminous Reality: The Poetry of Jorge Guillén* (see below). Relates the image of the circle to the idea of perfection and its antagonizing forces.

GIL DE BIEDMA, JAIME. *Cántico: El mundo y la poesía de Jorge Guillén*. Barcelona: Seix Barral, 1960. A useful study that includes material on stylistics and on the evolution of *Cántico*.

GONZALEZ MUELA, JOAQUIN. *El lenguaje poético de la generación Guillén-Lorca*. Madrid: Insula, 1954. On the stylistics of the Generation of 1927; frequent references to *Cántico*.

———. *La realidad y Jorge Guillén*. Madrid: Insula, 1962. A thematic study, with emphasis on the relationship between the poet and the outside world.

GULLON, RICARDO, and BLECUA, JOSE MANUEL. *La poesía de Jorge Guillén*. Zaragoza: Heraldo de Aragón, 1949. An early, still valuable, study of various aspects of *Cántico*. Published before the last edition of *Cántico* appeared.

HAVARD, ROBERT J. "The Early *décimas* of Jorge Guillén." *Bulletin of Hispanic Studies* 48 (1971): 111–27. A thematic and stylistic study of Guillén's early writing. Contains a valuable section on circular symbolism.

IVASK, IVAR. " 'Grand âge, nous ici': Some Remarks on the Theme of Old Age in Jorge Guillén's Poetry." In Ruiz de Conde, *Homenaje a Jorge Guillén* (see below). A brief overview of Guillén's treatment of the theme of aging; emphasis on *And Other Poems*.

———. "On First Looking Into Guillén's *Homenaje*." In Ivask and Marichal, *Luminous Reality: The Poetry of Jorge Guillén* (see below). A concise overview and summary of Guillén's third major work.

———. "Poesía integral en una era de desintegración." In Ciplijauskaité, *Jorge Guillén* (see above). A convincing argument on the permanence of Guillén's poetry in contrast to some extreme movements in twentieth-century literature.

———, and MARICHAL, JUAN, eds. *Luminous Reality: The Poetry of Jorge Guillén*. Norman: University of Oklahoma Press, 1969. A useful anthology of essays on various aspects of Guillén's work.

JIMENEZ, JUAN RAMON. "Crisis del espíritu en la poesía española contemporánea." *Nosotros* 48 (1940): 165–82. Jiménez's criticism of the Generation of 1927.

———. *Españoles de tres mundos*. Buenos Aires: Losada, 1942. Short essays on numerous literary figures.

———. *Selección de cartas*. Prologue by Francisco Garfias. Barcelona: Picazo, 1973. Includes correspondence with Guillén.

MACCURDY, G. GRANT. "Death in *Cántico:* Jorge Guillén and Martin Heidegger." *Romance Notes* (1982): in press. A comparison of the attitude toward death expressed in *Cántico* and the thought of the existentialist philosopher.

———. "The Erotic Poetry of Jorge Guillén's *Homenaje*." *Hispania* 65 (1982): in press. An analysis and thematic classification of the erotic poetry of this major collection.

———. "La estética y la psique: 'Bosque y bosque' de Jorge Guillén." *Explicación de Textos Literarios* 2 (1973): 75–79. A brief consideration of an archetypal pattern in Guillén's aesthetic outlook.

———. "Mandala: The Culmination of *Cántico*." *Hispanófila* 24 (1980): 57–69. A study of Guillén's geometrical imagery; emphasis placed on the archetypal foundation of this type of symbolism.

MACLEISH, ARCHIBALD. "Jorge Guillén: A Poet of This Time." *Atlantic Monthly*, January, 1961, pp. 127–29. An appreciation and overview.

MACRI, ORESTE. *La obra poética de Jorge Guillén*. Barcelona: Ariel, 1976. An overall survey of Guillén's poetry. All-inclusive to the point of becoming superficial.

MARAVALL, JOSE ANTONIO, ed. *Cuadernos Hispanoamericanos* 318 (1976): 495–649. A number of articles on different aspects of Guillén's work.

MARICHAL, JUAN. "The Spain of Jorge Guillén's Poetry." In Ivask and Marichal, *Luminous Reality: The Poetry of Jorge Guillén* (see above). A good summary of the intellectual ambience of the Generation of 1927.

MILLER, MARTHA LAFOLLETTE. "Transcendence Through Love in Jorge Guillén's *Cántico:* The Conciliation of Inner and Outer Reality." *Modern Language Notes* 92 (1977): 312–25. An illuminating study of the manner in which Guillén conceives of love as the vital link between the individual and the reality of the outside world.

MORRIS, C. B. *A Generation of Spanish Poets, 1920–1936*. Cambridge: Cambridge University Press, 1969. A thematic survey of the major works of the poets. Contains much interesting and valuable historical information.

ORTEGA, JOSE. "Conjunción y oposición en J. Guillén: De *Cántico* a *Clamor*." *Cuadernos Hispanoamericanos* 318 (1976): 542–49. A consideration of the shift in tone from one work to the other, based on textual interpretations.

PALLEY, JULIAN. "Jorge Guillén and the Poetry of Commitment." *Hispania* 45 (1962): 689–91. A brief study on the change from *Cántico* to *Clamor;* a valuable summary.

———. "The Metaphors of Jorge Guillén." *Hispania* 36 (1953): 321–24.

———. "Muerte a lo lejos." In *The Poem Itself,* edited by Stanley Burnshaw. New York: Holt, Rinehart and Winston, 1960. Commentary on Guillén's sonnet, "Death in the Distance."

PAZ, OCTAVIO. "Horas situadas de Jorge Guillén." *Papeles de Son Armadans* 40 (1966): 209–18. An appreciation of Guillén's vision of reality by this outstanding Mexican poet.

PINET, CAROLYN. "The Sacramental View of Poetry and the Religion of Love in Jorge Guillén's *Cántico*." *Hispania* 62 (1979): 47–55. A well-written study of religiosity in the metapoetic and erotic poetry of *Cántico*.

PLEAK, FRANCES AVERY. *The Poetry of Jorge Guillén*. Princeton: Princeton University Press, 1942. The first book in English on Guillén's poetry. Includes some translations.

POLO DE BERNABE, JOSE MANUEL. *Conciencia y lenguaje en la poesía de Jorge Guillén*. Madrid: Nacional, 1977. Excellent linguistic and stylistic analysis.

———. "Jorge Guillén: El poema como proceso de significación." *Explicación de Textos Literarios* 6 (1978): 199–203. Linguistic analysis.

POULET, GEORGES. *The Metamorphoses of the Circle*. Translated by Elliot Coleman and Carley Dawson. Baltimore: Johns Hopkins University Press, 1966. Contains a brief consideration of Guillén's circular imagery; emphasis placed on the primacy of the outside world.

PRAT, IGNACIO. *"Aire nuestro" de Jorge Guillén*. Barcelona: Planeta, 1974. An overview of Guillén's work; concentrates heavily on stylistics.

RODRIGUEZ, ISRAEL. *La metáfora en la estructura poética de Jorge Guillén y Federico García Lorca*. Madrid: Hispanova, 1977. Unrelated essays on Lorca and Guillén.

ROZAS, JUAN MANUEL, ed. *La generación del 27 desde dentro*. Madrid: Alcalá, 1974. An anthology of reminiscences by members of the Generation.

RUIZ DE CONDE, JUSTINA. *El cántico americano de Jorge Guillén*. Madrid: Turner, 1973. An anthology with critical commentaries and biographical details; based on Guillén's years at Wellesley College.

———. et al., eds. *Homenaje a Jorge Guillén*. Madrid: Insula (for Wellesley College), 1978. An anthology of essays on various aspects of Guillén's work.

SALINAS, PEDRO. *Literatura española, siglo XX*. 2d ed. Mexico City: Robredo, 1949. Contains essays on Guillén by his fellow poet and closest friend.

TORRE, GUILLERMO DE. *Historia de las literaturas de vanguardia*. 3 vols. 3d ed. Madrid: Guadarrama, 1974. A comprehensive study of numerous "isms" in contemporary literature.

VIDELA, GLORIA. *El ultraísmo: Estudios sobre movimientos de vanguardia*. Madrid: Gredos, 1963. The most thorough work on this movement.

WEBER, ROBERT J. "De *Cántico* a *Clamor*." *Revista Hispánica Moderna* 29 (1963): 109–19. A well-reasoned and well-documented attempt to date Guillén's shift from one work to the other, based on the dates of composition and subject matter of the poems added to the 1950 edition of *Cántico*.

WILSON, E. M. "Modern Spanish Poems: J. Guillén and Quevedo on Death." *Atlante* 1 (1953): 22–26. A brief comparison of the two poets.

YOUNG, HOWARD T. "Jorge Guillén and the Language of Poetry." *Hispania* 46 (1963): 66–70. A commentary (review article) on Guillén's principal critical work.

ZARDOYA, CONCHA. "*Clamor I:* Stylistic Peculiarities." In Ivask and Marichal, *Luminous Reality: The Poetry of Jorge Guillén* (see above). A stylistic analysis of *Sea of Confusion*.

———. *Poesía española contemporánea*. Madrid: Guadarrama, 1961. Essays on various themes favored by modern poets; contains explications of several poems by Guillén.

———. *Poesía española del 98 y del 27*. Madrid: Gredos, 1968. Essays on various figures from these two movements; contains a chapter on Guillén and Paul Valéry.

———. *Poesía española del siglo XX: Estudios temáticos y estilísticos*. 4 vols. Madrid: Gredos, 1974. A massive collection of essays on contemporary Spanish poetry; the three essays on Guillén (in vol. 2) originally appeared elsewhere.

ZULETA, EMILIA DE. *Cinco poetas españoles*. Madrid: Gredos, 1971. Contains an essay on the continuity of Guillén's affirmative vision in his work after *Cántico*.

2. Miscellaneous additional sources

ALLEN, RUPERT C. "Juan Ramón and the World Tree: A Symbological Analysis of Mysticism in the Poetry of Juan Ramón Jiménez." *Revista Hispánica Moderna* 35 (1969): 306–22. Valuable commentary on symbology and on tree symbolism is applicable to Guillén.

CHORON, JACQUES. *Death and Western Thought*. New York: Macmillan, 1963.

ELIADE, MIRCEA. *Yoga: Immortality and Freedom*. Translated by Willard R. Trask. New York: Pantheon, 1958.

GARCIA LORCA, FEDERICO. *Obras completas*. Edited by Arturo del Hoyo. Prologue by Jorge Guillén. 11th ed. Madrid: Aguilar, 1966.

GIBSON, IAN. *The Death of Lorca*. Chicago: J. Philip O'Hara, 1973.

HEIDEGGER, MARTIN. *Being and Time*. Translated by John Macquarrie and Edward Robinson. New York: Harper and Row, 1962.

JUNG, C. G. *Aion: Researches Into the Phenomenology of the Self. The Collected Works of C. G. Jung*. Vol. IX, part II. Translated by R. F. C. Hull. New York: Pantheon, 1959.

———. *Psychology and Alchemy. The Collected Works of C. B. Jung*. Vol. XII. Trans. by R. F. C. Hull. 2d ed. Princeton: Princeton University Press, 1968.

———. *Psychology and Religion: West and East. The Collected Works of C. G. Jung*. Vol. XI. Trans. by R. F. C. Hull. 2d ed. New York: Pantheon, 1963.

MOURANT, JOHN A. "*Scientia Media* and Molinism." *The Encyclopedia of Philosophy*. Vol. VII. Edited by Paul Edwards. New York: Macmillan, 1967.

NEUMANN, ERICH. *The Great Mother: An Analysis of the Archetype*. Translated by Ralph Manheim. 2d ed. New York: Pantheon, 1963.

NOSS, JOHN B. *Man's Religions*. 3d ed. New York: Macmillan, 1963.

SALINAS, PEDRO. *Poesías completas*. Edited by Soledad Salinas de Marichal. Prologue by Jorge Guillén. Barcelona: Barral, 1971.

SOBEJANO, GONZALO. *Nietzsche en España*. Madrid: Gredos, 1967.

TUCCI, GIUSEPPE. *The Theory and Practice of the Mandala*. Translated by Alan Houghton Brodrick. London: Rider, 1961.

Index